D0497163

PagePlus X6 User Guide

How to Contact Us

Our main office
(UK, Europe):

The Software Centre
PO Box 2000, Nottingham,
NG11 7GW, UK

Main: (0115) 914 2000

Registration (UK only): (0800) 376 1989

Sales (UK only): (0800) 376 7070

Customer Service/
Technical Support:
http://www.support.serif.com/

General Fax: (0115) 914 2020

North American office
(USA, Canada):

Serif Inc.,
The Software Center,
4041 MacArthur Blvd., Suite 120,
Newport Beach, CA 92660,
USA

Registration: (800) 794-6876

Sales: (800) 489-6703

Customer Service: (800) 489-6720

Technical Support: http://www.support.serif.com/

Online

Visit us on the web at: http://www.serif.com/

International

Please contact your local distributor/dealer. For further details, please contact us
at one of our phone numbers above.

Credits

This User Guide, and the software described in it, is furnished under an end user License Agreement, which is included with the product. The agreement specifies the permitted and prohibited uses.

Trademarks

Serif is a registered trademark of Serif (Europe) Ltd.

PagePlus is a registered trademark of Serif (Europe) Ltd.

All Serif product names are trademarks of Serif (Europe) Ltd.

Microsoft, Windows, and the Windows logo are registered trademarks of Microsoft Corporation. All other trademarks acknowledged.

Windows Vista and the Windows Vista Start button are trademarks or registered trademarks of Microsoft Corporation in the United States and/or other countries.

Kindle, the AmazonKindle logo, and Whispersync are trademarks of Amazon.com, Inc. or its affiliates.

Nook is a trademark of Barnes & Noble, Inc.

Copyrights

Digital Images ©2008 Hemera Technologies Inc. All Rights Reserved.

Digital Images ©2008 Jupiterimages Corporation, All Rights Reserved.

Digital Images ©2008 Jupiterimages France SAS, All Rights Reserved.

Bitstream Font content © 1981-2005 Bitstream Inc. All rights reserved.

Portions images © 1997-2002 Nova Development Corporation; © 1995 Expressions Computer Software; © 1996-98 CreatiCom, In.; 1996 Cliptoart; © 1997 Multimedia Agency Corporation; © 1997-98 Seattle Support Group. Rights of all parties reserved.

This application was developed using LEADTOOLS, copyright © 1991-2007 LEAD Technologies, Inc. ALL Rights Reserved.

Panose Typeface Matching System ©1991, 1992, 1995-97 Hewlett-Packard Corporation.

THE PROXIMITY HYPHENATION SYSTEM © 1989 Proximity Technology Inc. All rights reserved.

THE PROXIMITY/COLLINS DATABASE © 1990 William Collins Sons & Co. Ltd.; © 1990 Proximity Technology Inc. All rights reserved.

THE PROXIMITY/MERRIAM-WEBSTER DATABASE® © 1990 Merriam-Webster Inc.; © 1990 Proximity Technology Inc. All rights reserved.

The Sentry Spelling-Checker Engine © 2000 Wintertree Software Inc.

The ThesDB Thesaurus Engine © 1993-97 Wintertree Software Inc.

WGrammar Grammar-Checker Engine © 1998 Wintertree Software Inc.

Extensible Metadata Platform (XMP) Copyright © 2006 Adobe Systems Incorporated. All rights reserved.

In memory of Mike Koewler,
beta tester and long time supporter of Serif products.

Visual Reference

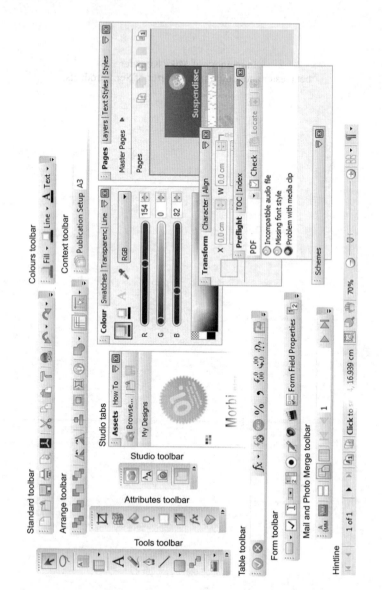

Standard toolbar

Arrange toolbar

Tools toolbar

Table toolbar

Form toolbar

Mail and Photo Merge toolbar

Hintline

Colours toolbar

Context toolbar

Studio tabs

Studio toolbar

Attributes toolbar

Table of Contents

Contents

1 Welcome

Welcome!

Welcome to **PagePlus X6**, the award-winning Desktop Publishing (DTP) solution from Serif. PagePlus is the easiest way to get superior publishing results, whether on your desktop or via professional printing. It's simple for anyone to create, publish and share their designs as outstanding printed documents, stunning PDFs, PDF slideshows, modern eBooks or via web page.

To make life so much easier, PagePlus comes with an impressive selection of design templates, creative content, and styles for you to use. As a result, publishing to a professional standard is easily achievable for experienced and inexperienced users alike! You'll also be able to reuse existing content by importing PDF documents and word processing documents. On the flipside, you'll be able to export drawn objects to all the latest graphic file formats.

PagePlus X6 doesn't stop at superior publishing. Its range of design studios makes PagePlus stand out from the crowd—**Cutout Studio** for cutting pictures out from their backgrounds, **LogoStudio** for custom logo design, and **PhotoLab** for powerful image adjustment and effect combinations. You simply cannot afford to miss them!

For a more detailed summary of what PagePlus can offer, see **Key features** (p. 4).

Upgrading?

If you've upgraded from a previous version, this new edition of PagePlus includes a host of **exciting new features** (p. 12) which keeps PagePlus ahead of its competitors and at a fraction of the price! We hope you also enjoy the additional power and performance edge.

Registration

Don't forget to register your new copy, using the **Registration Wizard**, on the **Help** menu. That way, we can keep you informed of new developments and future upgrades!

Key features

Before you get started with PagePlus, we recommend you take the opportunity to familiarize yourself with PagePlus key features and capabilities.

Layout

- **Versatile Setup with Auto-Imposition**
  Just click to specify layouts for small (business cards and labels), folded (booklets and greetings cards), and large publications (banners and posters)!

- **Ready-to-use Design Templates**
  Fancy a quick route to produce stunning designs for home or business use? Adopt one of an impressive collection of eye-catching **design templates**.

- **Theme layout design templates**
  Choose a **theme** on which to base your publication! Each theme offers a choice of publication types (**Brochure, Business Card, Flyer, Newsletter,** or **Poster**) and differently designed layout options for the theme. Pick **multiple layouts** as your new pages, then simply fill picture placeholders with your own pictures.

- **Master Pages**
  Save time and maintain consistency by using one or more master pages assigned to your publication pages. For more design freedom, **promote master page objects** to your page, making them detached and available for independent editing.

- **Layers**
  Each page can have multiple layers—so you can assign elements to different layers for modular design.

- **Professional layout tools**
  Movable **rulers, guide lines** and a **dot grid**, as layout aids, help you position objects precisely; snapping jumps an object to guide or grid. Use **Sticky guides**, a great way of moving (in bulk) all objects snapped to your guide lines—move the guide and objects will follow! Align and resize to objects using **Dynamic guide** snapping.

- **Page control**
  Add and remove pages in just a few clicks of your mouse in the Pages tab. Drag and drop pages within the tab to reorder sequence. Use **Mixed Page Orientations** to add landscape pages to your portrait-oriented publication, and vice versa. To view pages, **Multi-page view** lets you see an array of pages, even show a facing pages view!

- **Mail & Photo Merge**
  With Mail and Photo Merge, read data from just about any source: tables from HTML web pages, database files, even live ODBC servers! Print to labels and letters equally.

- **Tables and Calendars**
  Choose from a range of preset formats or design your own table. Use the convenient Table context toolbar to sort data, format cells, and choose from a wide range of functions for **spreadsheet calculations**. **Calendars** are table-based for enhanced functionality, and support Year update, inline personal events, and public holidays! Even create your own savable **table and calendar AutoFormats**.

- **BookPlus**
  Treat separate PagePlus publication files as chapters and use the BookPlus utility to link them into a book! Assign text styles and colour palettes across publications, automatically generate an Index or Table of Contents, add page numbering and output your final long document to both print and PDF.

- **Mixed Page Number Formats**
  Use different number formats (Arabic, Roman, or alphabetic) for your publication's front page, intro pages, table of contents, or index.

Pictures

- **Import Pictures**
  Import commonly-used standard file formats, including RAW digital camera formats. **AutoFlow** pictures (or drag and drop) into sequential **picture frames**! Import Adobe® Photoshop® files directly into your PagePlus publications.

- **Image Adjustments**
  Apply adjustments (**Brightness**, **Contrast**, **fix red eye**, and more) or use **Edit in PhotoPlus**, which accesses Serif's award-winning photo-editing package (if installed).

- **PhotoLab for non-destructive adjustment and effect filters**
  The powerful PhotoLab studio packs a punch with an impressive selection of editable adjustments, creative, and artistic effects (**pencil, water colour, oil**, and more). Use integrated **Straighten, Crop, Red-eye**, and **Spot-repair** tools for easy **retouching**. Apply filters to selected areas of your photo by using **brush-based masking**. Save adjustment/effect combinations as favourites for future use.

- **Quick-and-easy Cutouts**
  Cutout Studio makes light work of cutting out your placed pictures, directly in PagePlus. Use brushes to discard uniform backgrounds (sky, walls, etc.) or keep subjects of interest (people, objects, etc.).

- **A versatile Metafile Format**
  Import and Export Serif Metafiles (SMF), a proprietary image format with improvements to the Windows Metafile format (WMF). Better line, fill, and text definitions make them ideal for sharing graphics between Serif applications.

Creative

- **Drawing Tools**
  Design stunning vector graphics with **Pencil, Pen and Straight Line tools**, and add line endings like arrowheads, diamonds, and quills. Alternatively, the array of fully-customizable **QuickShapes** let you quickly create outlines for your designs, while **Convert to Curves, Crop to Shape**, and curve drawing offer complete flexibility for creating any shape imaginable! **Mesh warp envelopes** add perspective, slant, and bulge to any object. **Join object outlines** to create more complex outlined objects.

- **Fills and Lines**
  Enhance shapes, text frames, and artistic text with fantastic professional fills and lines. Use the Colour tab to change **fill, line, or text colour** with one click. Choose preset fills (solid, gradient, or bitmap) from the Swatches tab's palettes—even create stunning bitmap fills from your own images. What's more, every colour used is added to the **Publication Palette** so that you can easily re-use it again and again.

- **Intelligent Colour Schemes**
  Choose from dozens of preset colour schemes to change the overall appearance of your publications with a single click. You can customize the scheme colours or create your own schemes from **colour spreads** using **Colour Scheme Designer**.

- **Ready-to-use Styles**
  Choose various filter effects, glows, shadows, textures, and materials from the Styles tab. Customize the preset styles or store your own!

- **Transparency**
  Add transparency to your backgrounds, text frames, tables, shapes and text to achieve a truly professional look. As with colour fills, you can apply **solid**, **gradient**, and **bitmap** transparencies—even create bitmap transparencies from your own image collection.

- **Filter Effects**
  Apply eye-catching Filter Effects to make your images and text really stand out. Easily add shadows, glows, bevels, blurs, reflections, outlines, feathering, or embossing effects and alter the flexible settings for exactly the right look—your original object remains intact and editable if you change your mind! Use the **Shadow Tool** for on-the-page control of basic or skewed drop shadows.

- **Astounding 3D Lighting and Surface Effects**
  Advanced algorithms **bring flat shapes to life**! Choose one or more effects, then vary surface and multiple coloured light source properties. Start with a pattern or a function, adjust parameters for incredible surface contours, textures, fills, realistic-looking wood, water, skin, marble and much more. Combine 3D transparency and Reflection Maps for realistic glass-like effects on non-reflective/reflective surfaces.

- **Instant 3D**
  Transform your artistic text and shapes into impressive 3D objects directly on the page! Apply multiple coloured **lighting effects** (with directional control), along with custom **bevel** and **lathe** effect profiles to create your very own unique contours.

- **Connector Tools**
  Easily design **organizational charts**, **family trees** and other diagrams—connectors will link your boxes, circles, or other shapes together, with links being maintained during any object repositioning.

- **Stunning logos and flashes**
  Use pre-designed **ready-to-go logos**—alternatively, create from
  scratch in LogoStudio or base your design on existing PagePlus
  objects! Use **flashes** for poster advertising or greeting cards.

- **Decorative Picture Frames**
  Exciting ready-to-go picture frames can be applied around photos, text
  frames, and tables.

Text

- **Import text power!**
  Add word processing content to any text frame—**Word 2010** (and
  earlier versions), **Open Office**, **Rich Text Format**, PagePlus's
  WritePlus, and many more text formats.

- **Text Frames**
  Compose story text in **text frames** then easily position, rotate or size
  the frame to suit; connected frames host the same story text and can be
  filled automatically by **AutoFlow** or manual text fitting. Enhanced
  text wrap options and separate crop and wrap outlines mean you have
  greater control over where text flows and how it appears. Import,
  paste, export text in **Unicode** format... design with a foreign-language
  or special fonts and characters. **Text paths** also benefit from
  intelligent text fitting.

- **Anchor any object**
  Anchor **pictures, shapes, tables, artistic text,** and **nested text frames**
  to your publication's artistic or frame text. Position horizontally and
  vertically in relation to anchor point, indented text, column, frame,
  page margin guides, or the whole page. **Flow text** around floating
  objects in your text frame.

- **Text Control**
  Apply text formatting from an on-hand text context toolbar; apply
  multi-level bullet and numbering schemas to your paragraphs, even
  to your text styles; a Text Styles tab for allocating text attributes to
  chosen paragraphs; flexible bullet, numbering and indenting buttons;
  and much more!

- **Fonts**
  Substitute missing fonts when opening third-party publications or PDFs. View your currently installed font set in the Fonts tab, including those most recently assigned to text, favourite fonts, and those considered Websafe. Hover over a listed font for an "in-situ" **font preview** of your selected text—simply click to apply the new font if you like it! Easily **swap** all selected instances of a common font for another font in one fell swoop!

- **Professional-level OpenType Font Features**
  For advanced typography, PagePlus fully utilizes all your OpenType font features—**ligatures, stylistic sets/alternates, small/petite caps, case-sensitive forms, fractions, ordinals,** and many more are now available to both characters and text styles. You can now insert characters as glyphs, rather than Unicode characters!

- **Frame and Artistic Text**
  Create text with stunning transparency effects, gradient/bitmap (photo) fills, 2D/3D effects and more. Use designer **artistic text** for high impact headlines and powerful design elements—artistic text scales, flips, and can follow a drawn path, while **frame text** flows and line wraps.

- **Find & Replace**
  Search through story text for words and phrases but also text attributes, particular fonts, colours, special characters (Unicode), regular expressions, and words at specific positions in sentences.

- **Text Composition Tools**
  Includes **word count, spell-checking, thesaurus,** and **proof reader. Auto-Correct** and **Underline spelling mistakes as you type** proofing options are at hand.

- **Table of Contents & Index**
  Create automated **Table of Contents** and **Indexes** for complex documents. PagePlus refers to the named styles you've allocated to headings, subheadings and titles to automatically create your Table of Contents, with up to six levels. Indexing documents is simple too, use the intuitive tools to select important terms and let PagePlus do the rest.

- **Cross-references**
  Insert **cross-references** throughout your publication which reference **headings,** or **anchored text, tables, pictures,** or **diagrams** which

update automatically. Insert your cross-reference as a **page number**, **heading/anchor name, numbered list number**, and more. Add **Continued From/To cross-references** to text frames.

- **User-defined Variables**
  Set up your own **variables** to automatically update common terms that repeat throughout your publication. Great for updating product names, product versions, and language variants all at the same time.

Publishing and Sharing

- **PDF Import & Export**
  Import individual PDF pages or **whole PDF documents** as new PagePlus publications. Alternatively, **insert a PDF document's contents** into existing publications. Either way, PDF contents can be easily edited within PagePlus—the text and paragraph formatting of the original PDF document is maintained. **Export your documents to PDF**, with powerful options to publish your PDFs for professional printing (PDF/X) and the web (streaming supported). Scaling is supported.

- **PDF Forms**
  Create your own electronic **PDF form**, requesting information from form recipients. Your recipients can type in their responses, then save, print or submit their form electronically. Serif will email you completed forms, or you can set up your own web submission service.

- **PDF Slideshows**
  Create attention-grabbing **PDF slideshows** with stylish page and layer transitions—even add sound and movie clips! Share with friends, family, and colleagues. (See PagePlus Help.)

- **Colour Management**
  Set up **ICC profiles** for your monitor, printer and scanner, and be confident that your printed colours will closely match their appearance on-screen. Manage colour for multiple images with different embedded ICC profiles—allow or ignore image colour conversion to the document's working space. RGB and CMYK images display correctly to screen and print. For PDF printing, choose different **PDF/X1-a output intents** for **PDF colour management** in professional PDF publishing. Create accurate PDF output of greyscale images to **greyscale colour space**.

- **Printing**
  Print documents professionally on your home printer—as several pages on one sheet, or for large format printing, a single page across multiple sheets. For desktop printers without duplex support, use the **Manual Duplex** printing to create any double-sided publication. Print scaling is supported.

- **Interactive Print Preview with print-time imposition**
  Try out the exciting new **Print Preview**, packed with both preview and imposition options—create **books, booklets, thumbnails**, and **tiled** print output all **without prior page setup**. **Step&Repeat** and **N-up** options are also available.

- **Email your publications**
  Share your PagePlus documents natively or as HTML emails, complete with text, images, and active hyperlinks visible in the body of the email.

Management

- **Managing resources**
  List fonts, resources, and pictures used in your publication in the powerful **Resource Manager**. **Preview, relink, export**, and **replace** individual pictures and other resources. For fonts you can preview, check if embedded, locate **fonts** on the page, and export them.

- **Package your project**
  Gather together your project's supporting files to allow your project to be used on a different computer or at a print bureau. Resources such as fonts, linked graphics, linked media files, and more, are embedded in a project **package**—you'll never suffer from missing resources again!

- **Import Custom User Settings on Upgrade**
  Upgrading from PagePlus X5? Preserve your **custom Gallery content, object styles, preferences, user dictionaries, keyboard shortcuts, PDF profiles**, and much more—all from within PagePlus X6.

New features

Creative

- **Assets for a Creative Boost!** (see p. 67)
  Get creative with PagePlus's new **Assets tab**—the powerful new tab that lets you **browse and search** for professionally designed assets such as **graphics, picture frames, backgrounds,** as well as **mixed page content** and **entire pages**—all ready to drag and drop straight into your publication! The tab also lets you add pictures from your computer drive in readiness for use, and **store custom designs** for global or current publication use only. Finally, you'll be able to create **custom picture frames** and **backgrounds** from page objects!

Ease of Use

- **Clean Design—For Easier Page Development** (see p. 55)
  With Clean Design and dynamic guides working together, you'll get a clutter-free page layout combined with intelligent object-to-object positioning. Any placed guides, although hidden, can still be snapped to!

- **Multiple Tables of Contents with Easier Management** (see p. 165)
  Modern and truly interactive, the new **TOC tab** lets you create and manage multiple tables of contents. **Partial tables of contents** can also be placed at strategic points throughout your publication—great for complementing your main publication-wide TOC with **chapter-level TOCs** placed at chapter starts!

- **Indexing Made Easy** (see p. 169)
  Create, view, and manage index entries from one location—using the new **Index tab**. Mark all instances of the same word simultaneously for bulk indexing. As you build your index, generate your index from the tab again and again!

- **Business User Details per Publication!** (see p. 150)
  Create groupings of business user details, called **Business Sets**; apply a business set to each publication. Ideal for creating similar publications for different clients.

- **Multiple User Dictionaries**
  Use multiple user dictionaries—ideal for subject-specific sites (e.g., Medical or Legal). **Custom dictionaries** can be created for UK, US and many European languages, and can be applied selectively.

- **Improved Studio Tabs**
  A new **Studio** toolbar switches on/off **Assets tab**, **Fonts tab**, **How To tab**, or all tabs selectively. Individual tabs can be closed using an on-tab **Close** button—great for customizing your Studio tab **workspace**.

Design

- **PDF Interactivity** (see p. 241)
  For great-looking **PDF forms**, create **interactive buttons** that change in appearance on mouse click or rollover. Different colours, effects, or even pictures can be displayed in each "state". Hide and reveal selectable layers as a result of **different mouse actions**.

- **Access Streamed Media from Internet**
  Include streamed movies (MPEG, MP4, Shockwave, FLV, and QuickTime) or sound clips on your page.

- **New PANTONE PLUS SERIES**
  To add to PagePlus's already extensive PANTONE libraries, the **PANTONE PLUS SERIES** is now included, which is, in turn, complemented by the **PANTONE Goe™ System**.

- **Colours Toolbar for Easy Colour Assignment** (see p. 222)
  A new toolbar lets you apply **Fill**, **Line**, or **Text** colours from your current colour scheme or Publication Palette.

Printing and Publishing

- **PDF Preview** (see p. 253)
  Interactive Print Preview now allows for **PDF publishing**, with all the benefits of preview—imposition at publish time, scaling, page mark control, view controls, and of course a screen-wide representation of your intended PDF output.

- **Easy-to-use HTML Publishing** (see p. 270)
  Generate **web-ready pages** from your publication simply and with no fuss! Control hyperlink colours and background colour/image, as well as graphics export.

- **eBook Publishing** (see p. 266)
  Publish your eBook-optimized publication to **ePub** and share via desktop (Adobe Digital Edition), **tablet, android phone**, or **physical ePub devices**. For **Kindle** users, generate and launch .mobi eBooks directly from PagePlus. Add your own cover page and include your publication's table of contents.

- **Preflight Check for PDF, HTML and eBook Publishing** (see p. 262, p. 271, p. 268, respectively)
  Check your publication for potential publishing problems manually as you design and automatically as you publish. The **Preflight tab** displays, locates and fixes problems all in one go!

Advanced Publishing

- **Create Spot Colours** (see p. 223)
  For **Print** and **PDF publishing**, any publication colour can be made a **spot colour** using **Palette Manager**.

Installation

System Requirements

Minimum:

- Windows-based PC with DVD drive and mouse

- Microsoft Windows® XP (32 bit), Windows® Vista, or Windows® 7 operating system

- 512MB RAM

- 566MB free hard disk space

- 1024 x 768 monitor resolution (Use of Large Fonts may require a higher resolution)

Additional disk resources and memory are required when editing large and/or complex documents.

Optional:

- Windows-compatible printer

- TWAIN-compatible scanner and/or digital camera

- .NET 2.0 for text import filters (Word 2007/2010 + OpenOffice) (installed by default)

- Internet account and connection required for accessing online resources

First-time install

To install PagePlus X6 simply insert the PagePlus X6 program disc into your disk drive. The AutoRun feature automatically starts the Setup process. Just answer the on-screen questions to install the program.

Re-install

To re-install the software or to change the installation at a later date, select **Control Panel** from the Windows Start menu and then click on the **Programs - Uninstall a program** icon. Make sure the program disc is inserted into your drive, click the **Install...** button and then simply follow the on-screen instructions.

2 Getting Started

Startup Wizard

Once PagePlus has been installed, you're ready to start. Setup adds the program to your Windows **Start** menu.

- Use the Windows **Start** button to pop up the Start Menu, click on **All Programs**, and then click the **Serif PagePlus X6** item (or if PagePlus is already running, choose **New>New from Startup Wizard...** from the **File** menu).

On program launch, the Startup Wizard is displayed which offers different routes into PagePlus:

- **Start New Publication**, to open a blank page to work on.

- **Use Design Template**, to create an instant document from a pre-designed template.

- **Import PDF**, to create a publication from an existing PDF.

- **Download Free Stuff**, to access a range of free resources.

- **Visit Template Store**, to access the latest purchasable professionally design templates.

- **Open,** to access recently opened publications. Hover over each entry for a quick preview!

- **Learn,** to access online tutorial resources.

Use the **Choose Workspace** drop-down list to choose your workspace appearance (i.e., Studio tab positions, tab sizes, and show/hide tab status). You can adopt the default workspace profile <**Default Profile**>, the last used profile <**Current Profile**>, a range of profile presets, or a workspace profile you have previously saved.

> As you click on different profiles from the menu, your workspace will preview each tab layout in turn.

The Startup Wizard is displayed by default when you launch PagePlus. If you don't want to use the Startup Wizard again, enable the "Don't show this wizard again" option. You can switch it on again via the **Use startup wizard** check box in **Tools>Options...** (use Options>General menu option).

> You can also access the Startup Wizard at any time from **New>New from Startup Wizard...** on the **File** menu.

Creating a publication from a design template

PagePlus comes complete with a whole range of categorized design templates which will speed you through the creation of all kinds of publications for desktop or commercial printing!

Each template offers:

- **Complementary design**—Professionally designed layout with high-visual impact.

- **Schemes**—choose a named colour scheme to apply a specific look and feel.

Design templates come in two types—**theme layouts**, where you pick your own pictures, or ready-to-go **Pro templates** which are already populated with pictures.

Theme layouts offer a choice of themes (e.g., Ribbon) on which to base your publication (Brochure, Business Card, Flyer, Forms, Letterheads, Newsletter, etc.) ; you'll get picture placeholders instead of actual pictures. Simply add your own pictures to placeholders and personalize placeholder text, then publish.

You can also choose which page layouts you want to base your new publication on.

Ready-to-go Pro templates These are categorized templates containing royalty-free photos which can be adopted to fast-track you to your completed publication. You just need to personalize placeholder text, then publish.

To create a publication from a design template:

1. Open PagePlus, or choose **New...** from the **File** menu and select **New from Startup Wizard...**.

2. Click **Use Design Template** to display the Choose a Design Template dialog.

3. From the dialog, select a Theme Layout or a design template from the Pro Template Packs category. Select from the tree menu in the left-hand pane.

    Alternatively, simply choose a publication type from the same list, e.g. Brochures, Business Cards, etc.

4. Navigate the main window's categories and sub-categories using the ⊞ **Expand** and ⊟ **Collapse** buttons, then click your chosen thumbnail.

Theme Layouts   *Pro Design Templates*

5. Examine the page sample(s) on the right. For theme layouts with multiple pages (e.g., brochures), you can choose which pages you wish to be part of your publication by checking the check box under each page. For design templates, simply review the pages to be part of your publication.

Theme Layouts   *Pro Design Templates*

6. Pick a colour scheme from the drop-down list at the top of the dialog (the first three schemes are designed specifically for the chosen template). The page thumbnails refresh to reflect the new page's appearance. For a closer look, use the Zoom In/Zoom Out buttons or Zoom slider at the bottom of the dialog.

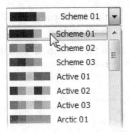

7. Click **OK**. The pages are added to your new publication.

All theme layouts contain assets, e.g. individual professional graphics, photos, photo frames, backgrounds, to complement your theme layouts.

Starting a new publication from scratch

Although design templates can simplify your design choices, you can just as easily start out from scratch with a new, blank publication. To make life easier you can adopt a particular document type (regular/normal, folded, small/large publication, web page) as a starting point.

To start a new publication (via Startup Wizard):

1. Open PagePlus to display the initial Startup Wizard (if switched on).
   - or -
   With PagePlus loaded, choose **New...** from the **File** menu and then select **New from Startup Wizard...**.

2. Select **Start New Publication**.

3. From the list on the left, select a document type and then examine the samples on the right. Click the sample that is the closest match to the document you want to create.
   - or -
   You can define a custom publication by clicking **Custom Page Setup...**.

4. (Optional) Select a **Theme** and colour **Scheme** for the publication from the respective drop-down lists at the top of the dialog. You can do this if you're familiar with PagePlus theme layouts and their associated colour schemes, and want to base your new publication on that scheme.

5. Click **OK** to open a new publication with a blank page.

At start up, if you click ![icon] (or press **Escape**) from the Startup Wizard, PagePlus opens a blank document using default page properties.

To start a new default publication:

-   Click ![icon] **New Publication** on the **Standard** toolbar (only if Startup Wizard is turned off).

Opening existing publications

You can open a PagePlus publication from the Startup Wizard, **Standard** toolbar, or via the **File** menu.

It is also possible to open PDF files as new publications, or Import PDF files and existing PagePlus files into currently open publications. (See PagePlus Help for both of these import options.)

To open an existing publication from the Startup Wizard:

1. From the Startup Wizard (at startup time or via **File>New**), review your publications from the **Open** section. The most recently opened file will be shown at the top of the list. To see a thumbnail preview of any file before opening, hover over its name in the list.

2. Click the file name to open it.

If your publication hasn't been opened recently, click ![icon] **Browse...** to navigate to it.

To open existing publications from within PagePlus:

1. Click  **Open** on the **Standard** toolbar.

2. In the **Open** dialog, select the folder and file name(s). For multiple publications, **Shift**-click to select adjacent multiple files or **Ctrl**-click to select non-adjacent files.

3. Click the **Open** button.

To open publications by drag-and-drop:

- From Windows Explorer, drag and drop the publication's preview thumbnail anywhere onto the PagePlus workspace.

To revert to the saved version of an open publication:

- Choose **Revert** from the **File** menu.

Font substitution

PagePlus supports automatic and manual font substitution if you open a publication which uses fonts which are not stored on your computer. See PagePlus Help for more details.

Working with more than one publication

If you have multiple publications open at the same time it's easy to jump between them using different methods.

| p123.ppp | **p456.ppp** × | p789.ppp * |

Click on an open publication's tab on the **Publications** toolbar at the top of the workspace to make it active (e.g., p456).

| 1 p123.ppp |
| ✓ 2 p456.ppp |
| 3 p789.ppp * |

Alternatively, you can select the name of a currently open publication from the **Window** menu. Unsaved publications are indicated by an asterisk; the currently active publication is shown with a tick.

Saving your publication

To save your work:

- Click 🖫 Save on the Standard toolbar.

- To save under a different name, choose Save As... from the File menu.

> 📌 Unsaved publications have an asterisk after their name in either the PagePlus title bar, publication tab, or Window menu.

Closing publications

To close the current publication:

- On the active publication's Publication tab, click the ✕ Close button.

- or -
Choose Close from the File menu.

To close PagePlus:

- Click the program's ✕ Close button at the top right of the window.

You'll be prompted to save changes to any unsaved publications.

3 Working with Pages

Setting up a publication

A publication's **page size** and **orientation** settings are fundamental to your layout, and are defined when the new publication is first created, either using a design template or as a New Publication choice via **File>New...** and the Startup Wizard. If the Startup Wizard is turned off, or you cancel the setup dialog, a new publication is created to a default page size.

To adjust size/orientation of the current publication:

1. Select   **Publication Setup** from the Pages context toolbar.

2. Ensure the **Paper** menu option is selected. The other option, **Margins**, lets you define non-printable Margin, Row, Column, and Bleed Guides as design aids. See Setting guides on p. 58.

3. For a **Regular/Booklet Publication**, you can select a pre-defined paper size, printer-derived paper size, or enter custom values for page **Width** and **Height**, as well as setting the orientation (Portrait or Landscape). For booklets only, select a type from the **Booklet** drop-down list, which page to start on (left/right), and if you require **Facing pages** (including **Dual master pages**). PagePlus automatically performs **imposition**. The settings ensure that two or four pages of the publication are printed on each sheet of paper, with pages printed following the booklet sequence. This saves you from having to calculate how to position and collate pairs of pages on a single larger page, and lets you use automatic page numbering for the booklet pages.

4. For other publication types, you can select: **Small Publications** (for example, business cards, labels, etc.), **Large Publications** (banners or posters), or **Folded Publications** (cards).

    *   For Small publications, enable **Paper** and choose a pre-defined option from the list, or for creating **Labels**, enable the radio button and pick an Avery label code which matches your labels.

    *   For Large and Folded publications, choose a pre-defined option from the list (use the preview).

5. Click **OK** to accept the new dimensions. The updated settings will be applied to the current publication.

For regular/booklet publications, you can also adopt printer-derived paper sizes that are supported by your desktop or network printer. These paper sizes will be different depending on which printer is currently chosen in the Print dialog. On the Pages context toolbar, these page sizes are indicated by the suffix "(From printer)" in the Paper size drop-down list.

Once you've set up your publication, you can optionally include repeated page elements on every page by creating master pages (p. 36).

Creating custom publication sizes

If the pre-defined options are not what you're looking for, you can customize any publication type to suit your requirements. You can base the custom publication on a pre-defined option by selecting the option in advance from the list.

Created from:	You'll need to:
Regular/Booklet	For regular publications: Select a page size, if you want Facing pages (with Dual master pages) and adjust Width/Height to suit; enable your preferred page orientation option (Portrait/Landscape).
	For booklets: As above, but choose a Booklet type as well.
Small	Select a Small publication type (card, tag, voucher, etc.), then click **Create Custom**. From the dialog, you can set:

- Size: The custom publication size.

- Gaps: The vertical and horizontal space between each "ganged" small publication.

- Margins: For custom Margins, override auto settings with Auto check box and set margins manually.

- Layout: Sets the number or small publications per page in an X/Y grid arrangement.

> For small publications, the dimensions are not only set via the Width
> and Height controls under **Size** but also depend on the values you use
> for **Gaps** and **Layout**.

Large
As for Small. Tile Overlap controls the how much printed pages overlap when output to standard printers.

Folded
Select a folding method from the list, then choose Width/Height for your publication size.

Facing pages

You can set up your regular publication or booklet so that the PagePlus window displays pages either singly or in pairs—as two facing pages side by side. You'll need facing pages if you're creating a publication where you need to see both the left-hand (verso) and right-hand (recto) pages, or one that employs double-page spreads where a headline or other element needs to run from the left-hand page to the right-hand page.

If you set up a publication to use facing pages, you can specify either a **single** or **dual** master page. A single master page is (as the name implies) a single page; a dual master page is a spread with both a left- and right-page component, allowing you to run elements across the spread in the background of the publication, or position left-side page numbers and right-side page numbers at opposite corners. The Pages tab shows single master pages with a standard page thumbnail, and dual master pages with a split-page thumbnail.

To set up facing pages for a regular publication or booklet:

1.   In the **Publication Setup** dialog, check **Facing Pages**.

2.   If you plan to use background elements that span a double-page spread, select **Dual master pages**. This will let you define master pages with paired "left page" and "right page" components.
     - or -
     For a facing-page layout where both left and right pages initially share the same master page, and you don't need to run background elements across the spread, clear **Dual master pages**.

Uniform and mixed page orientations

If you've changed your mind about the page orientation chosen at page setup, you can change the page orientation uniformly across your publication at any time.

PagePlus also lets you create a publication possessing a mixture of portrait and landscape page orientations. Changing a page's portrait orientation to landscape is especially useful when presenting a wide table, calendar, bar chart, or other graph.

To change all publication pages from portrait to landscape (or vice versa):

- From the Pages context toolbar, click the down arrow on the **Publication Orientation** button, then select **Landscape Publication** (or **Portrait Publication**) from the flyout.

To change a page from portrait to landscape (or vice versa):

1. In the Pages tab, double-click to select a page.

2. Click **Change page orientation** to swap between portrait and landscape orientation.
   - or -
   From the Pages context toolbar, click the down arrow on the **Page orientation** button, then select **Landscape Page** (or **Portrait Page**) from the flyout.

You can repeat the procedure for any other selected page.

You can also change the orientation of master pages using the equivalent **Change page orientation** on the Pages tab's Master Pages window.

This feature is only applicable for publications using standard page sizes (e.g., A4, A5, Letter, etc.)

Imposition

For press-ready output, you have the option to use **imposition** at the PDF or print stage, allowing you to create a folded publication (e.g., booklet or greeting card) from a non-folding publication without having to choose a folding publication in advance.

Adding, removing, and rearranging pages

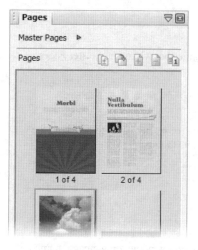

Use the **Pages tab** to add/delete standard or master pages, assign master pages to standard pages, and rearrange standard pages using drag-and-drop. You can also change page orientations.

The tab displays master pages in the upper **Master Pages** window (shown collapsed) and standard publication pages in the lower **Pages** window.

If a ready-to-go page layout is what you need, you can add extra pages from some themed layouts. See Adding additional pages on p. 35.

Page Manager provides additional options, such as copying a particular page's contents or adding/deleting multiple pages.

To add a single page:

1. On the **Pages** tab, click once to select a page in the **Pages** window. The thumbnail that's shown as "selected" is independent of the page you're currently working on. To work on a particular page, double-click its thumbnail.

2. Click **Add** to add a page (or master page) *before* the one selected in the window.
   - or -
   To add a new page *at the end* of the publication, deselect all pages by clicking in the neutral region of the lower window, then click the **Add** button.

To add master pages:

For master pages, the above procedure applies but within the Master Pages window.

To delete a single page/master page:

1. On the **Pages** tab, select the page (or master page) to delete on the appropriate window by clicking its thumbnail.

2. Click **Remove**.

To rearrange pages:

- On the **Pages** tab, in the lower **Pages** window, drag a page thumbnail over another page thumbnail in the page sequence. The page is added after the hovered over page thumbnail.

Adding additional pages

Use the Assets tab's Asset Browser if you're looking to use either some pre-designed pages or additional pages that complement your themed layout publication. See Browsing on p. 69.

Once in the Assets tab, you can add the page to your publication.

To add a page:

- Drag onto the currently viewed page to replace it.

- or -

- Drag to the left/right edge of the current page to place before or after. You'll see a Blue triangle to indicate before or after placement.

Understanding master pages

Master pages provide a flexible way to store background elements that you'd like to appear on more than one page—for example a logo, background, header/footer, or border design.

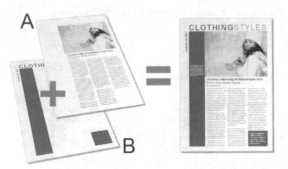

A - Page, B - Master Page

The key concept here is that a particular master page is typically **shared** by multiple pages, as illustrated below. By placing a design element on a master page and then assigning several pages to use that master page, you ensure that all the pages incorporate that element. Of course, each individual page can have its own "foreground" elements.

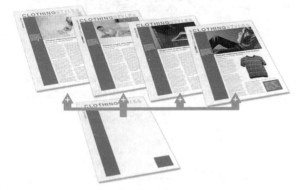

Master pages are available in every publication, but in a simple publication you may not need to use any master pages—or you may need only one master page. Facing pages and multiple master pages prove valuable with longer, more complex publications.

> If you're starting with a design template you may encounter one or more master pages incorporated with the design.

Using the **Pages** tab or **Page Manager**, you can quickly add or delete master pages; for example, you could set up different master pages for "title" or "chapter divider" pages.

Assigning master pages

If you're only using one master page it is assigned to any newly created page by default. However, if you're using multiple master pages you can assign a different master page to a standard page, all, odd or even pages. It's even possible to assign multiple master pages per page.

> You'll need to create an additional master page first. See Adding, removing, and rearranging pages on p. 33.

> Each new page or master page consists of a single layer; a page with a master page also shows the master page's Master Layer. One layer may be enough to accommodate the elements of a particular layout, but you can create additional layers as needed.

To assign a master page:

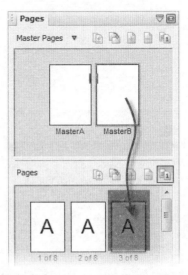

- From the expanded Master Pages window in the Pages tab, drag a master page onto a target standard page in the lower window.

  - or -

1. From the Layers tab, right-click a master layer and choose **Set Master Page...**

2. Select the page and the master page to be assigned to it.

Click 🔲 **Show Master Page Identifiers** to indicate the master pages used on the currently selected page(s). The master page is represented as a letter on the Page, e.g. A, B, C, etc.

To assign a master page to odd, even, or all pages:

- In the Pages tab, right-click the master page and choose an option from the **Apply to** submenu.

To disconnect a previously assigned master page(s):

- In the Pages tab, right-click in the Pages window and select **Remove Master Pages**.

Assigning multiple master pages

Just like a regular page, the master page can have its own set of layers associated with it, completely unique from the regular page! From the Layers tab, you'll see a master layer (e.g., Master Layer 1 [A]) as a separate entry. You can insert master layers from other master pages to assign additional master pages to your page.

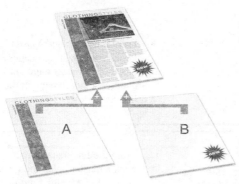

For an introduction to the concept of layers, see Working with layers on p. 45.

An additional master page needs to be created first. See Adding, removing, and rearranging pages on p. 33.

To assign multiple master pages to a page:

1. Display the page (not a master page) by double-clicking in the Pages tab.

2. On the Layers tab, select ⬚ **Add Master Layer**.

3. From the dialog, select the page from the **Select Master Page** box.

4. In the drop-down list, select the additional master page to be assigned.

5. (Optional) Enter a different name for your layer.

6. You can also modify layer properties as for standard layers.

7. Click **OK**.

To jump to a master page from the standard page:

- Double-click on a Master Layer entry in the Layers tab.
  - or -
  Right-click a master layer and choose **Go To Master Page**.

The master page assigned to the master layer is displayed.

An easy method for navigating from the selected master page to a last visited page is the **Return to** feature.

To jump to a page from a master page:

1. Select the master page in the Pages tab.

2. In the Layers tab, right-click any layer and choose Return to '*x* of *y*', where *x* is the last visited page and *y* is the total number of pages. The last visited page is displayed.

Facing pages and dual master pages

If you're using multi-page regular/booklet publications, you can assign different master pages to the left and right publication pages (also called spreads) if necessary—master pages are assigned per page and not per spread. For example (see below), a left-hand "body text" page might use the left-side component of one master page (**A**), while a right-hand page could use the right side of a different master page (**B**).

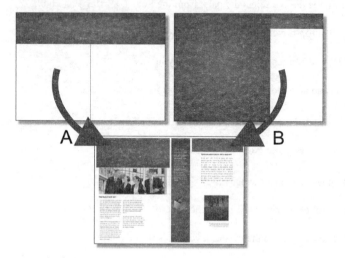

Editing master page objects

If you're editing pages which use master pages, master page objects will contribute to your page design. These objects can be edited quickly and easily from the page by using a control bar under the selected object.

To edit the master page object:

1. On your standard page, select the master page object, to reveal the control bar.

2. Click ⁺ᴬ **Edit on Master Page**. The master page is displayed for editing.

On occasion, you may want to make a master page object on your page independent from its master page. These objects can become editable by being **promoted** from the master page to the standard page, with the original master page object being replaced by a freely editable copy.

To promote a master page object:

1. On your standard page, select the master page object, to reveal the control bar under the object.

2. Click ⁼ᴬ **Promote from Master Page**. This makes a copy of the original object, which can then be edited independently without affecting the master page.

> 🖈 All other pages using the master page will remain unaffected.
>
> 🖈 Detaching a specific text frame will also detach any linked text frame associated with it. If the frames are on separate pages then all linked frames are placed on the same target page.

If you change your mind at any point you can reattach the object to the master page, leaving your page as it was originally.

To reattach object:

1. On your standard page, select the promoted object, to reveal the control bar under the object.

2. Click ⌄ᴬ **Revert to Master Page**.

Adding page backgrounds

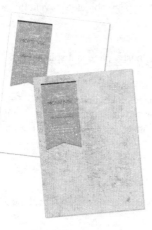

PagePlus provides a wide range of page backgrounds for your publication page. Backgrounds are assets (p. 67), which are available in Asset Packs such as Contemporary, Fun, Materials, and more.

To add a page background:

1. From the Assets tab, select **Browse...**.

2. In the **Asset Browser** dialog, select **Backgrounds** from the **Categories** section.

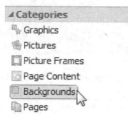

3. Navigate the Asset Packs to locate a background, then select an individual background or click **Add All** to include all the backgrounds from that pack. A check mark will appear on selected thumbnails.

4. Click **Close**. The background(s) will appear in the tab's Backgrounds category.

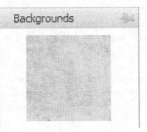

5. With the target page currently displayed, drag the background thumbnail onto the page.

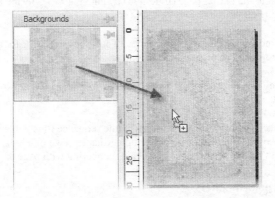

To store the background for reuse globally or just in the publication, drag to the Assets tab's My Designs or Backgrounds category. For the latter, If you close the publication, you'll be asked if you want to save the background to an asset pack. See Storing designs on p. 73.

Using page numbering

Page number fields automatically display the current page number. Typically, these fields are added automatically to the master page (so they appear on every page) with the Header and Footers Wizard (**Insert** menu), but you can insert a page number field anywhere in your text.

You can change the style of page numbers, create mixed page number formats, set starting page number(s), and control number continuation across chapters and publication sections (all via **Page Number Format** on the **Format** menu).

To insert a page number field:

1. Switch to the master page (if desired) by clicking 🔳 **Master Pages** on the Hintline.

2. With the **Artistic Text Tool** selected (**Tools** toolbar), click for an insertion point to place the page number.

3. On the **Insert** menu, select **Page Number** from the **Information** flyout.

You can also specify the **First Page Number** in the sequence (this will appear on the first page of the publication). For example, Chapter Two of a long publication might be in a separate file and begin numbering with page 33.

To set the first page number:

1. Uncheck **Continue from previous chapter**. PagePlus keeps this checked by default so that number continuation is maintained if your publication is to be part of a book.

2. Enter a different **First Page Number**.

For simple publications, it's likely that the same page format is used (e.g., Arabic numerals throughout). However, for more complex publications, different formats can be used for different page ranges, with each page range belonging to its own **publication section**. See PagePlus Help.

Working with layers

When you create a new publication from scratch or from a design template, the page(s) you create will initially consist of two **layers**—one for the page (Layer 1) and one for the associated master page (see p. 36), e.g., Master Layer 1 [A]. The layers can be seen within a hierarchical stack on the **Layers tab**.

One layer may be enough to accommodate the elements of a particular layout, but you can create additional layers as needed for the page. Layers are useful when you're working on a complex design where it makes sense to separate one cluster of objects from another. You can work on one layer at a time without worrying about affecting elements on a different layer.

If you frequently use the pasteboard, you'll notice pasteboard objects show under a special Pasteboard layer. This layer automatically disappears when you clear objects off the pasteboard.

A useful feature of the Layers tab is that you can see objects (and grouped objects) under the layer on which they were created. By expanding the layer by clicking ⊞, these objects are displayed—with a click, they can be selected on the page.

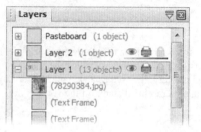

On each layer, objects such as text frames and pictures are stacked in the order you create them, from front to back, with each new object in front of the others. Layers themselves are stacked in a similar way, and of course you can juggle the order of objects and layers as needed. The uppermost layer is applied over any lower layer on the page.

Once you've displayed a page, you can normally edit any object on it—regardless of which layer the object is on—simply by clicking the object.

The above layer stack could represent the following:

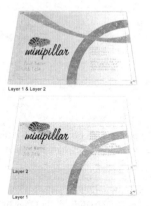

In order to create new objects on a particular layer, you'll need to select the layer.

To select a particular layer:

- Click a layer name. The layer entry then possesses a dark blue background.

The Master Layer entries work slightly differently to other layers. They indicate firstly that a master page and its layers are being used on the page, but also show the actual master page being used (MasterA is represented by the letter A on the layer entry). The master page's layers are not shown individually, but are combined into one thumbnail for clarity. However, you can display master page layers if required.

To display master page layers:

- Double-click the master layer entry. The Layers tab now shows the master page's layers. Note that the master page is now selected in the Pages tab.

For more information about master pages and assigning them to pages, see Understanding master pages on p. 36.

Adding, removing, and rearranging layers

Once you've created a page, it's easy to add, delete, move, or merge layers as needed. Moving a layer will place its objects in the front or back of those on other layers.

To add a new layer to the current page or master page:

1. In the Layers tab, click ✛ **Add Layer**.

2. You'll be prompted to give the new layer a name and set its properties. When you've made your selections, click **OK**.

The new layer is inserted above the currently selected layer. If a layer is not selected, the new layer is placed at the top of the stack.

To delete a layer:

- In the Layers tab, select the layer's name and click ▭ **Delete Selected Layers**.

You can also move, merge, and preview layers, as well as view layers with or without associated objects. (See PagePlus Help for more details.)

Layer names and properties

The Layers tab lets you rename layers and set a variety of properties for one or more layers.

To rename the layer:

1. In the Layers tab, click on the layer's name.

2. At the insertion point, type a new name then either press **Enter** or click away from the tab.

To set layer properties:

- Display the Layers tab.

Select desired settings for the selected layer.

- Click the ⬤ **Make Invisible** icon to hide the layer and any objects on it; click again to reveal the layer.

- Click the ▣ **Make Non-printable** icon to exclude the layer in page printouts; click again to include it. At print time, uncheck the **Print all layers** option in the Print dialog (Layers menu option) to exclude non-printable layers.

- Click the ▣ **Make Locked** icon to prevent objects on the layer from being selected/edited; click again to allow editing.

> You cannot select objects on a layer that is locked or not visible.

Double-click a layer or click ▦ **Layer properties** to change selection handle colour and extend settings to layers with the same name. See Layers tab in PagePlus Help.

Copying layers and objects

When you add a new page or master page to the publication, you can specify whether to copy the layers, objects, and/or the master page from a particular source page. See Adding, removing, and rearranging pages on p. 33.

Managing objects on layers

Objects can be managed in the Layers tab with various options for selecting, moving, and naming them.

Once you've displayed a page or master page, you can normally select and then edit any object on it—regardless of which layer the object is on—simply by clicking the object. Alternatively, you can limit object selection and editing to objects on a specific layer.

To edit only objects on the selected layer:

- In the Layers tab, click ![icon] **Edit All Layers**. When the button is disabled, editing is restricted to the selected layer only.

- Select the chosen layer, and its layer object, then edit.

PagePlus also gives you the option of selecting an object from the tab as opposed to from the page itself.

To select an object on a particular layer:

- In the Layers tab, click the ⊞ **Expand** on the chosen layer entry to reveal all associated objects. You'll see objects named automatically, e.g. "Line", "Quick Rectangle", IMG3445.jpg, etc., each with their own preview (hover over for a magnified view). The frontmost object in your drawing always appears at the top of the layer's listed objects (the order reflects the Z-order).

To select all objects on a particular layer:

- In the Layers tab, right-click the chosen layer and choose **Select Objects**.

To move an object to a specific layer:

- Drag the object(s) to a new position in the layer stack.

Objects are given default names when they are created (e.g., Text Frame, Picture), but can be renamed to make them more easy identify them from other layer objects. If a group is present it can also be assigned a more meaningful name.

To change an object's or group's name:

1. In the Layers tab, expand the layer entry to which an object or group belongs.

2. Select the object/group, then click on its name.

3. At the insertion point, type a new name then either press **Enter** or click away from the tab.

Viewing pages

Most of the PagePlus display is taken up by a page or "artwork" area and a surrounding "pasteboard" area.

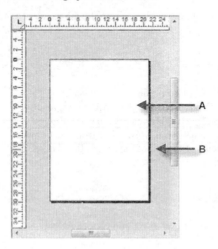

In PagePlus, the **Page** area (**A**) is where you add and position your text, shapes, and pictures that you want to print. The **Pasteboard** area (**B**) is where you generally keep any text, shapes, or pictures that are being prepared or waiting to be positioned on the page area.

To move or copy an object between pages via the Pasteboard:

1. Drag the object from the source page onto the pasteboard (hold down the **Ctrl** key to copy).

2. Use the page navigation buttons on the Hintline to jump to a target page.

3. Drag (or **Ctrl**-drag to copy) the object from the pasteboard onto the target page.

PagePlus makes it easy to see exactly what you're working on—from a wide view of multiple pages to a close-up view of a small region. For example, you can use the **scroll bars** at the right and bottom of the main window to move the page and pasteboard with respect to the main window. If you're using a **wheel mouse,** you can scroll vertically by rotating the wheel, or horizontally by **Shift**-scrolling.

Magnifying pages

For magnification options, the **Hintline** toolbar provides the:

Zoom to Current option to zoom to a selected object, or to the page width if no objects are selected.

Zoom Tool to zoom into an area defined by a drawn marquee selection.

Pan Tool for moving around the zoomed-in page area by dragging.

726% **Current Zoom** option to display or change the level of magnification. To change, click to select from a flyout or enter a custom percentage value directly.

Zoom Out and **Zoom In** tools so you can inspect and/or edit the page at different levels of detail. You can use the Zoom slider instead.

Navigating pages

To switch between pages:

- ◀ ▶ ◀ ▶ Click the **Previous Page**, **Next Page**, **First Page** or **Last Page** button on the Hintline.

  - or -

  Click in the **Current Page** box (e.g., 2 of 4) and type the page number you want to jump to.

  - or -

  On the Studio's **Pages** tab, double-click the page's thumbnail for the page (or master page) you want to view.

To switch between current page and its master page:

- From the Hintline toolbar, click 🔲 **Master Pages**.

4 Using Design Aids

Clean design

By default, PagePlus keeps its design aids hidden from view. This **Clean Design** feature is active while you design your publication, letting you work in a less cluttered workspace. You'll still have the option of switching off the feature, allowing you to view design aids—in reality, you'll probably want to switch in and out of Clean Design depending on your publication design.

Clean Design on (default) will display:	Clean Design off will display:
Spelling mistake underlines on text	Spelling mistake underlines on text
	Selection hover highlight
Selection hover highlight	Margin guides
Dot grid	Row and column guides
	Ruler guides
	Text frame/table boundaries

So how do I align objects if my guides or grid are hidden? Clean design operates with dynamic guides switched on, which means guides show between the dragged objects and already placed objects **as you drag objects**. This lets you align objects together by their edges, centres, and vertices. See Using dynamic guide on p. 56 for more details.

> Existing, but hidden, margin, row/column, and ruler guides are still offered as guides when Clean Design is enabled. You won't see them but they'll appear as any dragged object approaches them.

To switch off (on) clean design:

- Select ▥ **Clean Design** on the **Arrange** toolbar.

> Use **Ctrl-** as a keyboard shortcut to switch Clean Design on or off.

Dynamic guides

For accurate object alignment and resizing, you can use **dynamic guides** instead of setting ruler guides manually or performing selection, transform, and alignment operations. These red-coloured guides are shown between the vertices of the **last three selected** placed page objects and the manipulated object and "visually suggest" possible snapping options such as snap to the placed object's left, right, top, or bottom edge, or to the object (or page) centre. You can include objects to snap to by dragging over objects.

By default, dynamic guides are enabled, but they can be switched off (or back on again).

To switch off/on dynamic guides:

-  From the **Arrange** toolbar, click the down arrow on the **Snapping** button and click **Dynamic Guides** on the drop-down list.

To snap to page centres, you must additionally check **Page centre** from the same drop-down list.

Dynamic guides can be used either with or without Clean Design enabled.

Aligning objects

The use of dynamic guides is illustrated in the examples below. The darker object is already placed on the page, while the lighter object is being dragged into position.

Left   Right

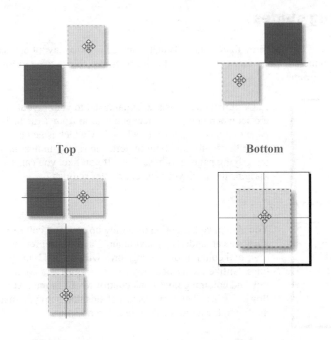

Top

Bottom

Object centre

Page centre

💡 You can also align using combinations of the above, e.g. right and bottom, depending on the position of your dragged object.

Resizing objects

The use of dynamic guides when resizing objects is illustrated in below. The darker object is already placed on the page, while the lighter object is being dragged into position.

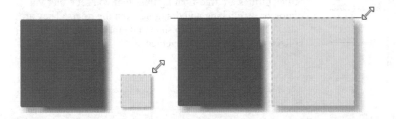

Setting guides

Guide lines are non-printable visual aids that help you position layout elements. They can include **page margins**, **row and column guides**, **bleed area guides**, and **ruler guides**.

Page margin settings are fundamental to your layout, and are set when you start a new publication from scratch. The page margins are shown as a blue box which is actually four guide lines—for top, bottom, left, and right—indicating the underlying page margin settings. If you like, you can set the margins to match your current printer settings.

You also have the option of setting up **row** and **column guides** as an underlying layout aid. PagePlus represents rows and columns on the page area with dashed blue guide lines. Unlike the dashed grey frame margins and columns, row and column guides don't control where frame text flows. Rather, they serve as visual aids that help you match the frame layout to the desired column layout.

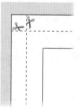

Bleed area guides assist you in positioning "bleed" elements that you want to run to the edge of a trimmed page. To allow for inaccuracies in the trimming process in professional printing, it's a good idea to extend these elements beyond the "trim edge"—the dimensions defined by your Publication Setup. With bleed guides switched on, the page border expands by a distance you specify, and the trim edge is shown with dashed lines and little "scissors" symbols. Note that these guide lines are just a visual aid; only the Bleed limit setting in the Publish as PDF or Print dialog extends the actual output page size.

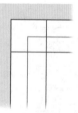

Ruler guides are free-floating lines that you set either via dialog or by clicking and dragging from the rulers. They are "sticky" so that objects can snap to them, then be moved collectively with guide movement.

If you're working in Clean Design mode (see p. 55), you won't see guides displayed on your page. You'll have to switch off Clean Design to see them.

Defining guide lines

To define margins, row/column guides, and bleed guides:

1. Select ⬜ **Publication Setup** from the Pages context toolbar.

2. In the dialog, select the **Margins** menu option to set guide lines for page margins, rows and columns, and bleed areas.

Creating ruler guides

PagePlus allows you to set up horizontal and vertical **ruler guides**—non-printing lines you can use to align headlines, pictures, and other layout elements.

To create ruler guides (via dialog):

1. Click ⬜ **Ruler Guides** on the Pages context toolbar.

2. (Optional) Choose the layer on which you want the ruler guides to be created. For multi-layered publications only.

3. Enter absolute guide positions in the Horizontal and/or Vertical boxes, clicking **Add** for each guide.

4. Repeat for the number of ruler guides you require.

5. Click **OK**. Your guides will appear on your page.

Guides can also be dragged onto the page if rulers are switched on.

To create ruler guides (by dragging):

- Click on a ruler, hold down your mouse button, then drag onto your page. A ruler guide line appears parallel to the ruler (**Alt**-drag to create the guide at 90 degrees to the ruler).

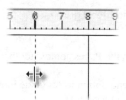

Managing guides

- To move row, column, or ruler guides, click and drag the guide.

- To remove a ruler guide, drag and drop it anywhere outside the page area.

- For precise ruler guide placement, check **Ruler marks** on the **Arrange** toolbar's **Snapping** menu to snap guides to ruler marks.

- Ruler guides are by default "sticky". 'Stuck' objects can be dragged around the page by their ruler guide—a great way to move previously aligned objects in bulk and simultaneously.

  To unstick a selected object, click one of two small red triangular markers shown at the point where the object is attached to the guide. You'll see a link cursor (⇐ ⇒) as you hover over the sticky guide marker.

- To turn sticky guides on and off, check/uncheck **Sticky Guides** from the **Arrange** menu (or the equivalent from **Tools>Options>Layout**). Previously stuck objects will remain sticky even after sticky guides are switched off—you'll have to make them non-sticky manually.

To hide or show guides:

- On the **View** menu, click **Guide Lines** from the **Grids and Guides** flyout.
- To hide/show bleed area guides, on the **View** menu, click **Bleed Area Guides** from the **Grid and Guides** flyout.

Using the rulers and dot grid

The PagePlus **rulers** mimic the paste-up artist's T-square, and serve several purposes:

- To act as a measuring tool.
- To create ruler guides for aligning and snapping.
- To set and display tab stops.
- To set and display paragraph indents (see p. 129).

Ruler units

To select the basic measurement unit used by the rulers:

- Right-click the  Ruler Intersection and set the measurement unit from the flyout.

The default unit is inches (US) or centimetres (international). If you plan to create HTML output, it's best to work in pixels as a measurement unit.

Adjusting rulers

By default, the horizontal ruler lies along the top of the PagePlus window and the vertical ruler along the left edge. The default **ruler intersection** is the top-left corner of the pasteboard area. The default **zero point** (marked as 0 on each ruler) is the top-left corner of the page area. (Even if you have set up bleed area guides and the screen shows an oversize page, the zero point stays in the same place, i.e. the top-left corner of the trimmed page.)

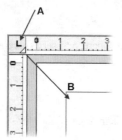

(A) Ruler intersection; (B) drag tab marker to set new zero point.

To define a new zero point:

- Drag the tab marker on the ruler intersection to a new zero point on the page or pasteboard. (Be sure to click only the triangular marker!)

To move the rulers:

- With the **Shift** key down, drag the tab marker on the ruler intersection. The zero point remains unchanged.

- Double-click on the ruler intersection to make the rulers and zero point jump to the top left-hand corner of the currently selected object. This comes in handy for measuring page objects.

To restore the original ruler position and zero point:

- Double-click the tab marker on the ruler intersection.

To lock the rulers and prevent them from being moved:

- Choose **Tools>Options...** and select the **Layout>Rulers** page, then check **Lock Rulers**.

Rulers as a measuring tool

The most obvious role for rulers is as a measuring tool. As you move the mouse pointer along the ruler, small lines along each ruler display the current horizontal and vertical cursor position. When you click to select an object, shaded ruler regions indicate the object's left/right and top/bottom edges on the horizontal and vertical rulers, respectively. Each region has a zero point relative to the object's upper left corner, so you can see the object's dimensions at a glance.

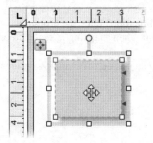

Using the dot grid

The **dot grid** is a matrix of dots based on ruler units, covering the page and pasteboard areas. Like ruler guides, it's handy for both visual alignment and snapping.

- To turn the dot grid on or off, click **Dot Grid** on the **View** menu's **Grids and Guides** flyout.

You can also set the grid spacing, style, colour, and positioning in the **Options** dialog (see PagePlus Help).

Snapping

The **snapping** feature simplifies placement and alignment by "magnetizing" moved or resized objects to grid dots and ruler guides. Objects can also snap to other guides on the page such as page margins, rows, columns, and bleeds (see p. 58), as well as the page edge, and page/margin centres (i.e., the centre of the page in relation to the page edge or page margins).

In addition, **dynamic guides** can be used to align and resize objects to existing object edges and centres by snapping. Guides appear dynamically as you drag objects.

To turn snapping on/off globally:

- Click ⬚ ▾ **Snapping** on the Hintline (don't click the drop-down arrow). The button has an blue colour when snapping is switched on.

Once snapping is enabled, you can selectively switch on/off snapping options (i.e., Ruler guides, Grid dots, etc).

To turn individual snapping controls on and off:

- Click the down arrow on the ⬚ ▾ **Snapping** button and check/uncheck a snapping option via the drop-down list.

Tools>Options offers the full set of snapping options for the user. You can control **Snapping Distance**, i.e. the distance in monitor pixels at which an object will start to snap to a dot, guide, etc, and **Nudging Distance**, i.e. the distance an object will move when using keyboard arrow keys to move it.

For precise ruler guide placement, check **Snapping>Ruler Marks** in **Tools>Options** to snap guides to ruler marks.

5 Assets for Creativity

Using assets

An **asset** is a general term for any object or page element that can be added to your page to enhance its appearance, increase efficiency, or personalize your design. Assets range from graphics, pictures, picture frames, and backgrounds, to more complex page content and entire pages.

To use assets, PagePlus provides the **Assets tab**, powered by both an Asset Browser (p. 69) and Asset Manager. The former browses your assets, the latter lets you create and manage custom Asset Packs.

Theme Layout design templates come complete with their own built-in assets, all themed to the publication's design. When you start from a theme layout the Assets tab will be populated with associated assets automatically!

Using the Assets tab

The Assets tab is a powerful design resource that exclusively hosts your browsed assets, ready for adding to your publication page.

Assets can be placed into the following categories.

- **My Designs**: Stores custom assets dragged from the page.

- **Graphics**: Stores professional clipart from Asset Packs.

- **Pictures**: Stores added pictures from your hard disk (or from Asset Pack, if containing pictures).

- **Picture Frames**: Stores picture frames from Asset Packs.

- **Page Content**: Stores page content (pre-assembled from various page objects) from Asset Packs.

- **Backgrounds**: Stores backgrounds from Asset Packs.

- **Pages**: Stores complete ready-to-go pages from Asset Packs.

The tab also lets you create custom designs for reuse globally or just in your publication. You'll be able to:

- Store your own designs to the tab's My Designs category for global use.

- Store your own designs to any other tab's category for current publication use.

- Create custom picture frames from drawn shapes.

- Create custom page backgrounds from pictures or filled page objects.

- Create custom page content (combinations of assets).

Although initially empty, the tab can be populated with assets of your choice by using an Asset Browser.

The Asset Browser

The Asset Browser lets you browse by asset category and Asset Pack (Pack Files), as well as search (by tag) for assets. Once displayed, the asset can be selected for inclusion in the Assets tab.

The Asset Manager

Use the **Asset Manager** to create your own Asset Packs by using assets from other Asset Packs and/or by importing pictures, graphics, or backgrounds. You can tag assets and then save or export your custom asset pack. See PagePlus Help for more information on creating custom Asset Packs.

Browsing

The **Asset Browser** offers a whole range of professional ready-to-go designs that you can use directly in your publication. These designs are provided in categorized Asset Packs installed with PagePlus. You can browse these packs and preview their contents, before adding assets to your workspace.

There are two ways to browse assets—by category or by Asset Pack (see p. 70). You can also use the search controls at the top-right of the dialog to narrow your search, or to find a specific asset.

To browse assets (by category):

1.   From the Assets tab, click 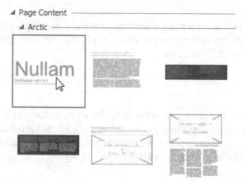 Browse....

2.   In the **Asset Browser**, select an asset category from the **Categories** section. You'll see installed Asset Packs appear in the main pane, stored under their Pack file names, e.g. Animals.

3.   Scroll through the asset packs to browse assets included in each pack.

To browse assets (by Asset Pack):

1.   From the Assets tab, click Browse....

2.   In the **Asset Browser**, on the left-hand side of the dialog, select an asset pack name from the **Pack Files** section, e.g., Backgrounds. The Asset Pack will appear in the main pane.

3.   The assets are categorized further in the main pane by the name of the Asset Pack to which they belong, e.g., Fun. Scroll through to browse the assets included in each Asset Pack. To make browsing easier, you can expand and collapse the Asset Packs to hide or reveal the assets.

4.   (Optional) To narrow your search, filter assets by entering an asset name in the **Search** box at the top-right of the main pane.

Searching for assets

The search facility filters assets based on preset and custom tags applied to all of the Asset Packs shown in the **Asset Browser**.

To apply a search filter:

- For a simple tag search, type the word or letter you want to search for in the **Search** text box, situated at the top right of the dialog. This is useful for retrieving assets with custom tags attached.

If your search results are being restricted to the currently highlighted category, Smart folder, Smart tag, or pack file, you can click the appropriate section header to remove the restriction.

Filtering assets

Filtering means that you can restrict the amount of assets on display.

- For category and/or pack file filtering, select a category or pack file (or multiple instances using Ctrl-click). You can also search for category and pack file combinations. For example, selecting the Picture Frames category and then a Theme Layout gives you just picture frames from that theme layout.

- For Smart tag filtering, select a tag name from the Smart Tags section. Smart tags let you filter assets logically by subject matter using a hierarchical and alphabetic tag structure. For example, if you select the "Occasions" tag you'll see all assets tagged with that tag; if you want Christmas-only assets, you could select "Christmas", nested under that Occasions tag.

- For single-tag filtering, select a tag
  name from the Tags section of the
  Asset Browser. (You may need to
  scroll down the left-hand pane to
  view). Use Ctrl-click to manually
  select multiple tags.

Adding assets to your Assets tab

To add a specific asset:

- Select the category or pack file in the Asset Browser, and then simply
  click the asset. A check mark shows on the thumbnail.

To add all assets:

- Click **Add All** from the upper-right corner of each Asset Pack's
  thumbnail gallery. Check marks will show on all thumbnails.

With either method, asset(s) will be available to you from the Assets tab when
you close the Asset Browser.

> Any asset stored in your Assets tab (but not added to the page) will be
> available to you the next time you open your publication. Assets can be
> made globally available by pinning in the relevant tab category. Custom
> designs can also be made global by dragging page objects to the tab's
> My Designs category.

Adding assets to your page

To add an asset to the page:

- Click its thumbnail in the design category and drag it out onto the page.

Storing designs

PagePlus lets you create custom assets to be used again, either just in your publication or globally in any publication in the future. Assets can be created and stored from objects already placed on the page. Example assets include:

- Graphics (from drawn vector shapes, line art, and artistic/frame text)

- Pictures (from adjusted or cutout pictures)

- Picture frames (from converted closed shapes, QuickShapes, and custom borders).

- Selected arrangement of page objects.

- Backgrounds (from converted pictures and filled objects).

- Publication pages.

At any time, designs are added by copying a design from the page to the Assets tab, then dragging it back onto your page where (and when) you want it.

Storing to My Designs

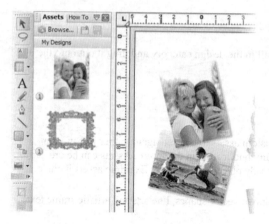

If you're keen on storing your own designs for **global** use, i.e. all publications, the Assets tab's **My Designs** category is ideal—designs will always be available in any new publication you create.

When you first install PagePlus, the My Designs gallery will be empty, ready for custom designs to be added to it.

To store a design in My Designs:

- Drag the object from the page and drop it onto the Assets tab's My Designs category. You don't need to expand the category in advance, as it will automatically expand for you.

If you drag to the Backgrounds or Picture Frames category, you'll convert the dragged object(s) to their respective asset type. For the former, you'll be prompted to create a background that will scaled or stretched to the publication's current page size. For the latter, any shape with an interior will convert to a picture frame (with placeholder).

Saving My Designs

Any designs you store in your My Designs category will be saved as a My Designs.ppack file to your Windows Application Data folder.

Storing Pages

Any page present in your publication can be stored in the Assets tab (Pages category).

To store a page:

1. From the Assets tab's Pages category, click **Add...**.

2. From the dialog, check a page (or master page) that exists in your publication.

3. Click **OK**.

Storing to other categories

Designs can also be added to other categories, but will only be available to the current publication (unless pinned—see p. 76). Typically, you can store vector shapes, line art, artistic text, and text frames in the Graphics category, unless you want to make it globally available via the My Designs category.

When you close your publication, any custom design you've stored in these categories will need to be saved. You'll be prompted to save the design to a custom Asset Pack specific to the publication.

To save a design to other categories:

- Drag the object from the page and drop it onto any other category.

Pinning categories and individual assets

Individual assets and entire categories within the Assets tab can be made available for all documents (i.e., globally) if they are pinned.

Assets can only be pinned if they have been saved as part of an asset pack. If you attempt to pin an unsaved asset, you will be prompted to save your asset pack.

To pin and unpin assets:

- To pin all the assets in a category, click **Pin All** on the category header.
  - or -

  To pin an individual asset, click the icon on the individual asset.

- To unpin all the assets in a category, click **Unpin All** on the category header.
  - or -

  To unpin an individual asset, click the icon on the individual asset.

6 Working with Objects

Selecting an object

Before you can change any object, you need to select it using one of a choice of tools on the **Tools** toolbar.

 Pointer Tool
  Click to use the **Pointer Tool** to select, move, copy, resize or rotate objects.

Lasso Tool
  Click to use the **Lasso Tool** to draw a freeform region under which any objects will become selected.

Prior to any selection, PagePlus objects will display a "glowing" selection hover highlight around the object. In a complex grouping of objects, this indicates which object will become selected.

To select an object:

- Click on the "glowing" object using one of the tools shown above, to reveal a bounding box around the object.

If objects overlap, click on the overlapping area until the "hidden" object is selected.

For more precise object selection, you can draw an irregular-shaped lasso around one or more objects in a complex design.

To select an object with the Lasso Tool:

1.   Select the ⌒ **Lasso Tool**.

2.   Draw a "lasso" around the object(s) you want to select. A shaded lasso region is created around the object.

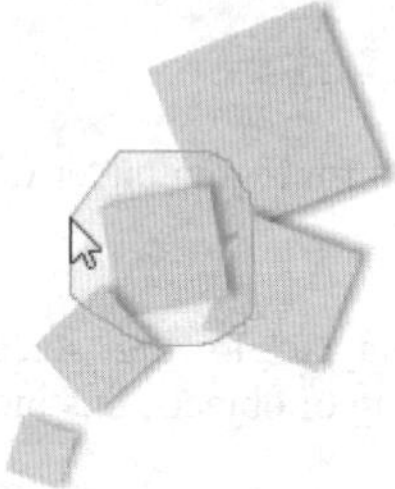

3.   Release the mouse button. All of the objects within the lasso region are selected.

If attempting to lasso an object within a group, remember to ungroup the objects first.

To avoid picking up an object under your cursor, keep the **Shift** key pressed as you draw the lasso.

If you prefer to keep the Pointer Tool selected, you can lasso objects as described above with the **Alt** key pressed.

To select a text object with the Pointer Tool:

•   Clicking on a text object (artistic text or text frame) with the Pointer Tool selects the object and also positions the blinking text selection cursor within the object's text. In this mode, you can edit the text (see p. 126).

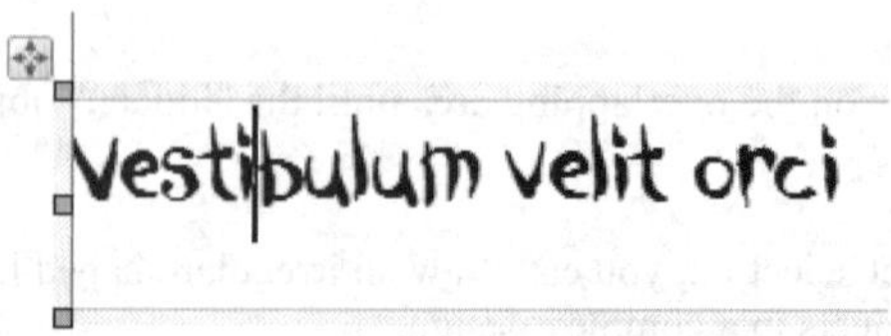

Vestibulum velit orci

- Double-, triple-, or quadruple-click to select a word, paragraph, or all text.

- To select only the text frame, click the frame's bounding box.

- Clicking on a group selects the grouped object. **Ctrl**-click to select an individual object within a group.

Selecting multiple objects

Selecting more than one object at a time (creating a **multiple selection**) lets you:

- Position or resize all the objects at the same time.

- Create a **group object** from the multiple selection, which can then be treated as a single object, with the option of restoring the individual objects later. See Creating groups on p. 85.

To create a multiple selection:

- Drag a "marquee" box around the objects you want to select.

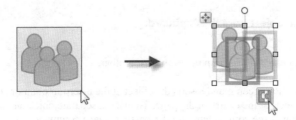

Alternatively, either hold down the **Shift** key and click each object in turn, or use the Lasso Tool (p. 80) to draw around objects to select them.

To add or remove an object from a multiple selection:

- Hold down the **Shift** key and click the object to be added or removed.

To deselect all objects in a multiple selection:

- Click in a blank area of the page.

To select all objects on the page (or master page):

- Choose Select>Select All from the Edit menu (or press Ctrl+A).

Copying, pasting, and replicating objects

Besides using the Windows Clipboard to copy and paste objects, you can duplicate objects easily using drag-and-drop, and replicate multiple copies of any object in precise formations. You can also transfer the formatting of one object to another, with the option of selecting specific attributes to be included when formatting is pasted.

To copy an object (or multiple selection) to the Windows Clipboard:

- Click Copy on the Standard toolbar.

If you're using another Windows application, you can usually copy and paste objects via the Clipboard.

To paste an object from the Clipboard:

- Click Paste on the Standard toolbar.

The standard Paste command inserts the object at the insertion point or (for a separate object) at the centre of the page. To insert a separate object at the same page location as the copied item, use the Paste in Place command.

To choose between alternative Clipboard formats:

- Choose Paste Special... from the Edit menu.

To duplicate an object:

1. Select the object, then press the **Ctrl** key.

2. Drag the object via the 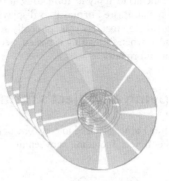 **Move** button to a new location on the page, then release the mouse button.

3. To constrain the position of the copy (to same horizontal or vertical), also press and hold down the **Shift** key while dragging. A duplicate of the object appears at the new location.

Replicating objects

Duplicating an object means making just one copy at a time. The **Replicate** command lets you create multiple copies in a single step, with precise control over how the copies are arranged, either as a linear series or a grid. You can include one or more transformations to produce an interesting array of rotated and/or resized objects. It's great for repeating backgrounds, or for perfectly-aligned montages of an image or object.

To replicate an object:

1. Select the object to be replicated and choose **Replicate...** from the **Edit** menu. The Replicate dialog appears, with a preview region at the right.

2. To arrange copies in a straight line, select **Create line**. For an X-by-Y grid arrangement, select **Create grid**.

3. Specify **Line length** (the number of objects including the original) in the arrangement, or the Grid size. Note that you can use the Line length setting to include an odd number of objects in a grid.

4. Set spacing between the objects as either an **Offset** (measured between the top left corners of successive objects) or a **Gap** (between the bottom right and top left corners). You can specify **Horizontal** and/or **Vertical** spacing, and/or an angular **Rotation**. To set a specific

horizontal or vertical interval, check **Absolute**; uncheck the box to specify the interval as a percentage of the original object's dimensions.

5. Click **OK**.

The result is a multiple selection. Click its  **Group** button if you want to keep the separate objects linked for additional manipulations.

Pasting an object's formatting

Once you have copied an object to the Clipboard, you can use **Paste Format** (**Edit** menu) to apply its formatting attributes to another object. Again from the **Edit** menu, **Paste Format Plus** displays a "master control" **Style Attributes Editor** dialog that lets you optionally select or deselect specific attributes to be included when formatting is pasted. See Saving object styles on p. 216 for more dialog information.

Copying an object's formatting

Format Painter is used to copy one object's line and fill properties directly to another object, including between line/shape and text objects.

To apply one object's formatting to another:

1. Select the object whose formatting you wish to copy.

2. Click **Format Painter** on the **Standard** toolbar. When you click the button, the selected object's formatting is "picked up".

3. Click another object to apply the first object's formatting to it. The second object becomes selected.

4. To select another object without pasting the formatting, click it with the **Shift** key down.

5. To cancel Format Painter mode, press **Esc**, click on a blank area, or choose any tool button.

For copy formatting from one text object to another, a number of other text properties (font, style, and so on) besides line and fill are passed along at the same time.

Creating groups

You can easily turn a multiple selection into a group object. When objects are grouped, you can position, resize, or rotate the objects all at the same time.

To create a group from a multiple selection:

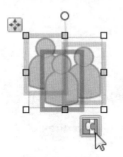

- Click the **Group Objects** button.

To ungroup:

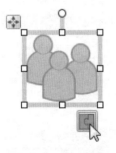

- Click the **Ungroup Objects** button. The group turns back to a multiple selection.

Simply clicking on any member of a group selects the group object. In general, any operation you carry out on a selected group affects each member of the group. However, the objects that comprise a group are intact, and you can also select and edit an individual object within a group.

To select an individual object within a group:

- **Ctrl**-click the object.

Moving objects

To move an object (including a multiple selection):

- Drag the selected object by using its 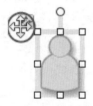 **Move** button. Once you see a move cursor over the button you can begin dragging.

> To set exact horizontal and vertical positions, use the Transform tab.

To constrain the movement of an object to horizontal or vertical:

- Select the object and use the keyboard arrows (up, down, left, right).

Resizing objects

PagePlus provides several methods for resizing single or grouped objects. Click-and-drag is the simplest—watch the Hintline for context-sensitive tips and shortcuts.

To resize an object (in general):

1. Select the object.

2. Click one of the selection handles and drag it to a new position while holding down the left mouse button.

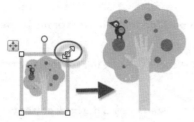

Dragging from an edge handle resizes in one dimension, by moving that edge. Dragging from a corner handle resizes in two dimensions, by moving two edges.

> Text in frames and tables doesn't change size when the container object is resized.

> To set two or more objects to the same horizontal or vertical size as the last selected object, you can use **Arrange>Size Objects....**

> You can also make fine resizing adjustments from the Transform tab.

To resize freely:

*   Drag from a corner (or line end) handle.

To constrain an object's dimensions when resizing:

*   Hold the **Shift** key down and drag from a corner (or line end) handle.

For shapes, this has the effect of keeping a square as a square, a circle as a circle, etc.

> For pictures, dimensions are constrained on dragging a corner handle. Use **Shift**-drag to resize a picture freely.

Ordering objects

On each layer, objects such as text frames, graphics, and photos are stacked in the order you create them, from back to front, with each new object in front of the others. You can change the stacking order, which affects how these objects appear on the page.

To shift the selected object's position to the bottom or top of the stack:

- Click ⬛ Send to Back or ⬛ Bring to Front on the Arrange toolbar, respectively.

To shift the object's position one step toward the back or front:

- Click ⬛ Back One or ⬛ Forward One on the Arrange toolbar, respectively.

For complete control while ordering objects, the Layers tab lets you drag and drop an object to any position in the stack within the layer, but also to a new position in a different layer.

To order objects via the Layers tab:

- From the Layers tab, drag an object to its new position. A green line indicates the object's new position when you release the mouse button.

Aligning and distributing objects

Aligning and distributing objects gives your project a polished feel. With PagePlus, you can align your objects in relation to each other or the page using dynamic guides or the Align tab.

Aligning with dynamic guides

As you draw, you can align your object using dynamic guides. By default, these red-coloured guides show as you draw or position your object. With dynamic guides, you can align your object in relation to other objects' top, bottom, left or right edges or their centre. For more information on how to use them, see Dynamic guides on p. 56.

Aligning with the Align tab

Alignment involves taking a group of selected objects and aligning them all in one operation by their top, bottom, left or right edges. You can also distribute objects, so that your objects (as a multiple selection) are spread evenly (optionally at spaced intervals).

Alignment or distribution can occur between the endmost objects on your page (current selection), page margins, or page edge. For example, with multiple selected objects, aligning to Top aligns all objects to the topmost edge of the highest object; align to Bottom aligns all objects to the bottommost edge of the lowest object.

Alignment relative to the last selected object lets you choose a specific object in a multiple selection from which to align other objects.

To align the edges of two or more objects in a selection:

1.   Using the Pointer Tool, **Shift**-click on all the objects you want to align, or draw a marquee box around them, to create a multiple selection.

2.   Select the Align tab.

3.   Select an option for vertical and/or horizontal alignment. Choose **Top, Bottom, Left, Right, Centre Horizontally** or **Centre Vertically,** i.e.

To distribute two or more objects across a selection:

• Choose 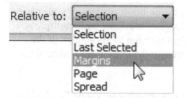 **Space Evenly Across** or   **Space Evenly Down** to spread selected objects uniformly between endmost objects in the current selection (horizontally or vertically, respectively) or by a set measurement (choose **Spaced** and set a value in any measurement unit).

Rather than work within the current selection area you can align or distribute to page margins (if set) or page edge.

To align/distribute objects to page margins, edges, or across page spreads:

Relative to:	Selection ▼
Selection
Last Selected
Margins
Page
Spread

• Select from the **Relative to** drop-down list to align the selected object(s) within the page **Margins**, **Page** edges, or **Spread** (for facing pages) then choose an align or distribute button described above.

For more advanced alignment control, you can align multiple objects in relation to your last selected object (select objects in turn with the **Shift** key pressed) by using the **Relative to: Last Selected** drop-down list option.

The last selected object is shown with a darker bounding box when compared to other selected objects.

Exporting as a picture

Exporting as a picture lets you convert all the objects on the page, or just the currently selected object(s), to an image file, using a file format you specify.

To export as a picture:

1. (If exporting objects, not the whole page) Select the object or **Shift**-click (or drag a marquee) to select multiple objects.

2. Choose **Export As Picture...** from the **File** menu.

3. In the **Save as type** drop-down list, select a image format, e.g. **Serif MetaFile Format (*.smf)**.

4. Specify a folder and file name for the picture.

5. To export just selected object(s), check **Selected object(s)**. To export the whole page, uncheck this box.

6. To choose from export options such as resolution, colour, and transparency, check **Show filter options**.

7. Click **Save**. You'll see export options, if available and requested, for the particular export filter in use.

Exporting Serif Metafiles

PagePlus lets you export pictures in Serif Metafile Format (SMF). This proprietary format, an improvement on the Windows Metafile Format (WMF) due to improved text, line and fill handling, is especially useful for interworking between Serif products, i.e. you may want to utilize PagePlus objects in another Serif application to save time and effort. The object is converted to a graphic and becomes non-editable, but the object's original appearance will be honoured.

Rotating an object

You can rotate single and multiple objects, including pictures, text objects, and groups using the object's rotation handle or the Pointer Tool.

To rotate a selected object (using its rotation handle):

- Click and drag the rotation handle extending from the selection box (use the **Shift** key while dragging for 15° rotation intervals).

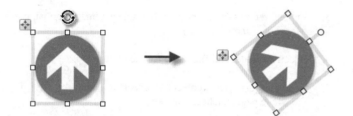

To rotate an object (using Pointer Tool):

1. Select the **Pointer Tool** on the **Tools** toolbar.

2.   Click to select the object, hover over one of its edge or corner handles until you see the rotate cursor.

3. Hold the mouse button down and drag the cursor in the direction in which you want to rotate the object, then release (use the **Shift** key for 15° rotation intervals).

To undo rotation (then restore the original orientation):

- Double-click the object's rotation handle.

- To restore the rotated position, double-click the rotation handle again.

To change the rotation origin:

1. Select the ![Pointer Tool icon] **Pointer Tool** and click to select the object.

2. Click the object's rotation handle.

3. Move the rotation origin ⊕ away from its original position in the centre of the object to any position on the page. The origin can also be moved to be outside the object—ideal for rotating grouped objects around a central point.

4. Drag the rotation handle to a new rotation angle—the object will rotate about the new origin.

To reset the rotation origin, simply double-click it.

To rotate an object 90 degrees left or right:

- Select the object and click ![Rotate Left icon] **Rotate Left** or ![Rotate Right icon] **Rotate Right** on the **Arrange** toolbar.

Flipping an object

You can flip objects horizontally (left to right; top and bottom stay the same) or vertically (top to bottom; left and right stay the same).

To flip an object horizontally/vertically:

- Select the object and choose **Flip Horizontal** or **Flip Vertical** from the **Arrange** menu.

Cropping and combining objects

Cropping means masking (hiding) parts of an object, for example to improve composition or create a special effect. The underlying object remains intact. Two types of cropping are possible—**square** cropping or **irregular** cropping.

square crop   *irregular crop*

Combining starts with more than one object, but creates a special composite object with one or more "holes" on the inside where the component objects' fills overlapped one another—useful for creating mask or stencil effects.

To crop using the object's original outline:

1. Select the object, then select the ▢ **Square Crop Tool** on the **Attributes** toolbar.

2. For a vector object (shape, line, etc.), drag one of its edge or corner handles inward for unconstrained cropping; press the **Shift** key while dragging for constrained cropping (aspect ratio is maintained). For pictures (above), the crop operation is constrained by default.

> To scale the object within the crop outline, press the **Ctrl** key, click your left mouse button, then move your mouse upwards or downwards.

To crop by modifying the object's outline:

- Select the object and select the [⬜] **Irregular Crop Tool** on the **Square Crop** context toolbar. The Curve context toolbar appears on its right, which lets you control the displayed nodes and connecting segments that define the object's crop outline. See Editing lines on p. 202.

  - To move a node (control point) where you see the $-\vdash-$ cursor, drag the node.

  - ⌐⌐ To move a line segment (between two nodes) where you see the cursor, drag the segment.

To position a cropped object within its crop outline:

- With either crop tool selected, click the object and drag its centre (when you see the hand cursor).

To feather the crop outline:

- With either crop tool selected, click the object.

- From the Crop context toolbar, set a **Feather** value using the up/down arrows, slider or by direct input. Feathering is applied outside the crop outline by the set point size.

To uncrop (restore full visibility):

- Click the [🗔] **Remove Crop** button on the **Square Crop** context toolbar.

Cropping one shape to another

The **Crop to Shape** command works with exactly two objects selected. Either or both of these may be a group object. The lower object (the one behind the other) gets clipped to the outline of the upper object, leaving a shape equivalent to the overlapping region.

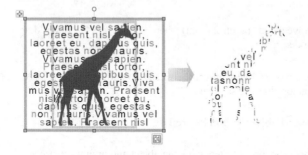

To crop one shape to another:

1. Place the "clipping" object in front of the object to be cropped, using the **Arrange** menu and/or **Arrange** toolbar as needed.

2. With both objects selected (or grouped), choose **Crop to Shape** from the **Tools** menu.

You can restore an object cropped in this way to its original shape, but the upper "cropping" object is permanently deleted (use **Undo** to recover it if necessary).

Combining lines and shapes

Combining curves is a way of creating a composite object from two or more lines or drawn shapes. As with cropping to a shape, the object in front clips the object(s) behind, in this case leaving one or more "holes" where the component objects overlapped. As with grouping, you can apply formatting (such as line or fill) to the combined object and continue to edit individual nodes and segments with the **Pointer Tool**. Unlike those other methods, a combined object permanently takes the line and fill properties of the front object. Combining is reversible, but the component objects keep the line and fill properties of the combined object.

Combining is a quick way to create a mask or stencil cutout:

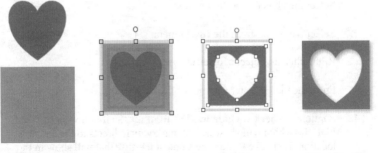

| *QuickShapes* | *Convert to Curves* | *Combine Curves* | *Drop Shadow Added* |

To combine two or more selected lines or drawn shapes:

1. Draw your two lines or QuickShapes.

2. Place the "clipping" object in front of the object to be cut out.

3. Select each object and choose **Tools>Convert To>Curves** for both.

4. Select both objects.

5. Choose **Combine Curves** from the **Arrange** menu.

To restore the original shapes from a combined object:

*   Select it and choose **Split Curves** from the **Arrange** menu.

Adding anchors to objects

Anchors can be added to objects to allow hyperlinks and cross-references to link directly to a specific location rather than to the whole page. This is especially useful if you're referring to a page object such as an image or table, or to selected artistic or frame text.

Named anchors can optionally be included as PDF bookmarks. The anchor's name is added automatically to the PDF bookmark list as a new bookmark title; after generating your PDF, the bookmark can be clicked to navigate to that anchor location.

To add an anchor:

1. Select the object or portion of text.

2. Select **Anchor...** from the **Insert** menu.
    - or -
    Right-click an object and select **Insert Anchor...**.

3. From the dialog, enter a name for the anchor.

4. (Optional) Check **Include in PDF Bookmarks** if you want to create a PDF file which will show a bookmark which directs to the anchor's location. If checked, enter the **Bookmark title** that will show in the generated PDF.

5. Click **OK**.

Once created, you can insert hyperlinks, cross-references, and PDF bookmarks, directly linked to the new anchor.

To delete an anchor:

1. Select the object which has an anchor that you wish to remove.

2. Click **Anchor...** from the **Insert** menu (or **Insert Anchor...** from the right-click menu).

3. In the dialog, click **Delete**.

4. From the next dialog, you can either leave or delete all bookmarks or hyperlinks to the anchor independently of each other. Click Yes or No as appropriate.

Anchoring objects to text

If you're working with text frames you'll probably want to add supporting shapes, pictures, tables, or even nested text frames within your publication's text (artistic or frame text). Such objects can be positioned either in relation to a position in your text (or other page element) or be simply placed inline in your text. In either instance, objects can then move with the text as you add further text content.

In PagePlus, this positioning is controlled by **anchoring** an object using different positioning options.

- **Float with text**. ⚓ The object is positioned horizontally and vertically relative to an **anchor point**. This option is ideal for pictures, pulled quotes, etc.

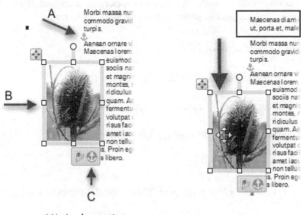

(A) Anchor point,
(B) Anchored object,
(C) Anchor properties

Pasted text causes reflow

- **Position inline as character**. The anchored object is placed as a character in the text and aligned in relation to the text that surrounds it. The anchored object flows with the text as before.

- **Detach from text**. The anchored object is disconnected from its anchor point, leaving a normal unanchored object.

PagePlus objects can be anchored to anywhere in your publication text, but the floated object can be positioned in relation to indented text, column, frame, page margin guides, the page itself, or most typically the anchor point in a text frame.

For text frames, when the text reflows, the anchor point (and therefore anchored object) reflows with the text. This allows supporting anchored objects to always stay with supporting text as more text is added to the frame.

To create an anchored object:

1. Position your unanchored object on the page.

2. Select **Anchor Object...** from the **Arrange** menu.

3. From the dialog, choose a positioning option:

Either, for a **floating** object:

1. Enable **Float with text**. This is the default positioning option.

2. Click **OK**. The ⚓ 🔵 **Anchor point** appears and your object is now an anchored (showing an icon).

Or, for an **inline** object:

1. Enable **Position inline as character**.

2. Click **OK**. 🔵 The object appears inline with text, and shows an **Anchor Properties** icon.

Objects inserted into text frames will automatically be anchored using "Float with text" default settings. However, the anchored object can be dragged away from the anchor point as an alternative method for creating an anchored object.

To view anchor properties:

1. Select an anchored object.

2. Click ⬤ **Anchor Properties** shown under the object.

The **Anchored Object Properties** dialog is displayed. The options differ depending on which of the three positioning options is enabled.

If you'd like to change the position of an anchor point you can drag it anywhere else in your text frame. Dragging to an area of no text will disconnect your anchored object. You can also disconnect the anchor point via Anchor Properties dialog.

To disconnect an anchored object:

*   Enable **Detach from text**.

The Anchor Properties button and anchor point both disappear.

> Anchored object have all the same properties of unanchored objects; you can modify them whilst anchored.

> Frame text can wrap around floating anchored objects, as described in Wrapping text (p. 140). Inline anchored objects do not allow text wrapping.

Joining object outlines

PagePlus includes some powerful tools to carve new shapes out of old overlapping shapes. With add, subtract, intersect, or exclude commands you actually produce a permanent new object (with a new outline) out of any selected objects. The joined object can be further edited by adjusting nodes in the new shape.

To join outlines:

1. Select objects.

2. Select an outlines option from the ⬛ **Join Outlines** flyout on the **Arrange** toolbar.

Add	Creates one new object that's the sum of any two selected objects.

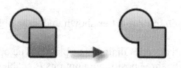

> The objects need not be overlapping.

Subtract	Discards the overlap between the top and bottom object. The top object is also discarded. Useful as a quick way of truncating shapes and pictures with another object.

> Ensure the objects are overlapping!

Intersect	Retains the overlap and discards the rest.

Exclude	Merges two or more objects into a composite object, with a clear transparent "hole" where their filled regions overlap.

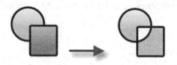

Applying a mesh warp envelope

Mesh warping lets you apply a preset warp envelope to your PagePlus object or bitmap (below), then optionally modify a flexible grid of points and lines that you can drag to deform or distort an object and (optionally) its fill.

To apply a basic mesh warp to a selected object:

1. Select the object, then select the ![icon] **Mesh Warp Tool** on the **Attributes** toolbar.

2. Select a warp from the **Preset Warps** flyout on the Mesh Warp context toolbar.

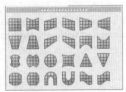

    The object deforms accordingly and a simple mesh outline appears around the object, with a node at each corner or around its outline.

3. You can use the Mesh Warp context toolbar to:

    *   **Disable Warp** temporarily.

    *   Choose a different **Preset Warp**.

    *   Specify with **Warp Fills** whether or not the warp effect extends to the object's gradient or bitmap fill or the bitmap's pixels.

Once created, selecting an existing envelope will activate the Pointer Tool (for manipulating the object), When you click on a node, the context toolbar lets you modify the selected node.

To enable a warp after disabling:

- Select the 🪟 **Mesh Warp Tool** on the **Attributes** toolbar.

The process of editing mesh warps and their envelopes is described in greater detail in the PagePlus Help.

Adding logos

Logos are intended to send a clear message to your target audience, all within a simple and identifiable design. Whether you intend to communicate a stylish, business, fun or modern message (opposite), PagePlus allows you to create impressive logos of varying design.

Logos are great for adding to master pages associated with any publication.

To add a logo:

1. From the Assets tab, select 📷 **Browse....**

2. In the **Asset Browser**, scroll the left-hand pane, and select **Logos** from the **Pack Files** section.

3. 🔘 Navigate the thumbnails in the right-hand pane and select an individual logo or click **Add All** to include all the logos. A check mark will appear on selected thumbnails.

4. Click **Close**. The logo(s) appears in the tab's Graphics category.

5.   Drag a chosen logo thumbnail to your page.

6.   From the **Insert Logo** dialog, you can choose design variations, add a name or motto and apply colours, i.e.

   - **For design variations:** Select a design from the **Designs** pane (e.g., offering different text labels and positions).

   - **For a name or motto**: You can add a name or motto to your logo in their respective text fields.

   - **For colour**: To apply the publication's current colour scheme to your design, uncheck **Apply colour set**. Alternatively, to adopt a colour set independent of your publication's current colour scheme, keep **Apply colour set** checked and pick a colour set option from the drop-down list.

7.   Click **OK**.

Flashes, used for celebratory and promotional messages, can also be created using the same process as adding logos except you select "Flashes" instead of "Logos" from the Asset Browser's Pack File location.

If you're looking to further modify your logo you can use **LogoStudio**, an integrated design environment. This allows you to focus on your design without the distractions of other objects on the page, i.e. the design is displayed in isolation and centred on the page. Alternatively, a logo or flash can be created from existing artistic text, shape, asset, picture, or grouped objects.

To edit an existing logo:

1.   Click the ![button] button on the control bar under the selected logo.

   LogoStudio is launched with your object(s) zoomed in to fit your workspace.

2.   Using standard PagePlus tools and tabs, customize your logo design to your liking.

3.   Click ![close icon] **Close LogoStudio** from LogoStudio's main toolbar to exit. The modified logo is updated in its original position.

Converting objects to logos

It's just as easy to by-pass the pre-defined logos and base your custom logo on objects already present in your publication or website. The logo can be converted back to separate objects at any time by ungrouping.

To convert existing objects to a logo:

1. Select one or more objects (or a grouped object) on the page.

2. Select **Edit in LogoStudio...** from the **Edit** menu (or select via right-click).

3. Edit your logo design. In particular, you can use the upper **Logo Text** input box to "caption" your logo (typically a company or club name), then click the tick box.

Inserting media clips

You can insert media into your publication which will play in your published PDF file or HTML output. Your PDF file could be a PDF slideshow, PDF form or a more simple PDF document. Each type of clip can be placed in a particular position on your PagePlus document's page, and, when exported as PDF, the clip can be clicked for playback. Media clips can be great accompaniments to your promotional, email, or e-learning material!

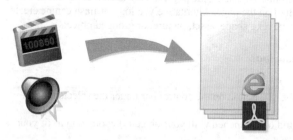

A variety of commonly used formats are supported, including both **non-streaming** and **streaming** media.

> Non-streaming files must download in entirety to a user's computer before they begin playing; streaming files require a special player that buffers incoming data and can start playing before the whole clip has arrived.

Most media clips can be either linked or embedded when the clips are stored locally; clips accessed via URL can only be linked. When **embedding**, the source file is stored in your publication, as opposed to keeping it separate when linked. Although embedding any file adds to the size of the publication, it is the default option because you'll no longer have to worry about juggling separate files or the chance of accidentally deleting one of them. When you publish, some streaming media must be embedded; PagePlus will warn you of this via the Preflight tab.

The visitor will be able to trigger the playback of a given media file by clicking an icon or picture pre-linked to the media file. A media "player" will be visible on your published page.

To insert media clips (via icon or picture):

1. Choose ![icon] **Sound Clip** or ![icon] **Movie Clip** from the **Media Clip>** flyout, located on the **Insert** menu.
   - or -

   If you're designing a form, pick the same options from the **Forms** toolbar.

2. From the dialog, add a **Title** for the media clip. This is for your reference only, and is not displayed.

3. Select your media location, either available locally (**Media**) or via the Internet (**URL**).

   - Enable **Media**, then navigate to the folder location of the media file, and select the file. Click **Open**.

     - or -

   - Enable **URL**, then enter (or type) the absolute web address for the file. You could paste in the file's URL, if it already exists on the Internet—ensure you copy the exact URL of the file rather than that of just the website.

4. If you do not wish to embed the file in your publication, uncheck **Embedded**.

5. For playback, set the playback to **Loop** or play **Once**; include playback controls alongside your placed clip (check **Show Player Controls**). Optionally, include the playback control in a **Floating window** (if checked).

6. Check the **Locked** option to prevent the clip from being altered in the PDF output.

7. In the Appearance tab, use the **Visibility** option to show a media clip's border, and set the thumbnail border's width, style, and colour.

8. From the Poster section, select a graphic to use as a picture thumbnail instead of the standard sound or movie thumbnail. For movies, a poster thumbnail can be generated from the original movie file by enabling **Retrieve from media**.

9. Click **OK**.

10. Position the cursor over a point on the page, and either:

    • To insert the clip's thumbnail at a default size, simply click the mouse.
      - or -

    • To set the size of the inserted thumbnail, drag out a region and release the mouse button.

You can then position the icon on your page. When the document is exported your media content is ready to be played!

To change a clip's properties:

• Right-click on the clip thumbnail, and choose **Media Clip Properties....**

Updating and saving defaults

Object defaults are the stored property settings PagePlus applies to newly created objects such as:

- **lines** and **shapes** (line and fill colour, shade, pattern, transparency, etc.)

- **frames** (margins, columns, etc.)

- **text** (i.e., font, size, colour, alignment, etc.). Defaults are saved separately for **artistic, shape, frame** and **table text.**

You can easily change the defaults for any type of object via the **Update Object Default** command or the **Text Style Palette** dialog.

Default settings are always **local**—that is, any changed defaults apply to the current publication and are automatically saved with it, so they're in effect next time you open that publication. However, at any time you can use the **Save Defaults** command to record the current defaults as **global** settings that will be in effect for any new publication you subsequently create.

To set local defaults for a particular type of object:

1. Create a single sample object and fine-tune its properties as desired—or use an existing object that already has the right properties. (For graphics, you can use a line, shape, or rectangle; all share the same set of defaults.)

2. Select the object that's the basis for the new defaults and from the **Format** menu, select **Update Object Default**.

Or, for line and fill colours, including line styles:

1. With no object selected, choose the required line and/or fill colours from the Colour or Swatches tab. Use the Line tab to set a default line weight, style, and corner shape.

2. Draw your object on the page, which will automatically adopt the newly defined default colours and styles.

To view and change default text properties:

1. From the **Format** menu, select **Text Style Palette...**.

2. Double-click **Default Text**, then from the expanded list of text types, choose an option (e.g., Artistic Text).

3. Click **Modify...** to view current settings for the selected text type.

4. Use the Text Style dialog to alter character, paragraph, or other properties.

To save all current defaults as global settings:

1. From the **Tools** menu, select **Save Default Settings...**.

2. From the dialog, check options to update specific defaults globally:

    - **Document and object defaults** - saves current document settings (page size, orientation) and object settings (context toolbar settings).

    - **Text styles** - saves current text styles in the Text Style Palette.

    - **Object styles** - saves user-defined styles from Styles tab.

    - **Table and calendar formats** - saves custom formats saved in Table Formats dialog.

3. Click **Save** to confirm that you want new publications to use the checked object's defaults globally.

7 **Working with Text**

Understanding text frames

Typically, text in PagePlus goes into **text frames**, which work equally well as containers for single words, standalone paragraphs, multipage articles, or chapter text.

> You can also use artistic text (see p. 122) for standalone text with special effects, or table text (on p. 158) for row-and-column displays.

What's a text frame?

A text frame is effectively a mini-page, with:

- Margins and column guides to control text flow.

- Optional preceding and following frames.

- Text and optional inline images that flow through the frames.

The text in a frame is called a **story**.

- When you move a text frame, its story text moves with it.

- When you resize a text frame, its story text reflows to the new dimensions.

Frames can be linked so that a single story continues from one frame to another. But text frames can just as easily stand alone. Thus in any publication, you can create text in a single frame, spread a story over several frames, and/or include many independent frame sequences. By placing text frames anywhere, in any order, you can build up newspaper or newsletter style publications with a story flowing from one column to another (below) or even across pages.

Frame 1   *Frame 2*

Creating text frames

You add text frames and position them on the page as you would any other object, in advance of adding text content.

To create a frame:

1. Select   **Standard Text Frame** from the **Tools** toolbar.

2. Click on the page or pasteboard to create a new frame at a default size.
    - or -
    Drag out to place the text frame at your chosen dimensions.

> Once created, your frame edges will be hidden on deselection of the frame because **Clean Design** is switched on. The edges will be shown on frame hover over. Frame text will always be shown.

To delete a frame:

*   Select the frame—click its edge until a solid border appears—and then press the **Delete** key.

You can select, move, and resize text frames just like other objects (see p. 79, 86, and 87, respectively). When you select a frame's bounding box, indicated by a solid border line plus corner and edge handles, you can manage the frame properties; selecting inside a frame creates a blinking insertion point in the frame's text (the frame's boundary box becomes hatched to indicate editing mode). In this mode, you can edit the text. (For details, see Editing text on the page on p. 126.)

PagePlus also lets you create a wide variety of shaped frames from closed shapes or QuickShapes (see p. 204).

To create a frame (from a shape):

1. Draw a shape with a line tool or create a QuickShape.

2. Select **Convert To>Shaped Text Frame** from the **Tools** menu (or right-click).
    - or -
    Type directly onto the QuickShape to automatically create a shaped frame.

Putting text into a frame

You can put text into a frame using one of the following methods:

WritePlus story editor: With a selected frame, click **[AI]** **Edit story in WritePlus** on the Frame context toolbar.

Importing text: Right-click on a frame and choose **Insert Text File...** to import text.

Typing into the frame: Select the Pointer Tool, then click for an insertion point to type text straight into a frame, or edit existing text. (See Editing text on the page on p. 126.)

Pasting via the Clipboard: At an insertion point in the text, press **Ctrl+V**.

Drag and drop: Select text (e.g. in a word processor file), then drag it onto the PagePlus page.
If you drop onto a selected frame, the text is pasted inline where the insertion point had been placed previously. Otherwise, a new frame is created for the text.

Frame setup and layout

The **frame layout** controls how text will flow in the frame. The frame can contain multiple **columns**. When a frame is selected, its column margins appear as dashed grey guide lines if set in **Frame Setup**. Note that unlike the page margin and row/column guides, which serve as layout guides for placing page elements, the frame column guides actually determine how text flows within each frame. Text won't flow outside the column margins.

You can drag the column guides or use a dialog to adjust the top and bottom **column blinds** and the left and right **column margins**.

(A) Column margins, (B) Column blinds

To edit frame properties directly:

- Select the frame object, then drag column guide lines to adjust the boundaries of the column.

(1)   *(2)*   *(3)*

The frame edge is clicked to show a **selected** bounding box (**1**), after dragging inwards the column margin can be adjusted (**2**), and after dragging downwards, the top margin blind can be moved (**3**).

To edit frame properties using a dialog:

1. Select the frame and click [icon] **Frame Setup** on the Frame context toolbar.

2. From the dialog, you can change the **Number of columns**, **Gutter** distance between columns, **Left Margin**, **Right Margin**, and enable/disable text wrapping around an object.

3. To change the column widths and blinds (top and bottom frame margins), click a cell in the table and enter a new value.

How a story flows through a sequence of frames

You can have just one frame on its own, or you can have many frames. Frames can be connected in linked **sequences** so that the **story** associated with a given frame sequence flows through the first frame on to the next and keeps flowing into frames in the link sequence.

A key difference from a word processor is that PagePlus does not normally add or remove frames according to the amount of text. The text simply flows until the text runs out (and some frames are left empty), or the frames run out (and some text is left over), i.e.

- If the text runs out before the last frame, you have some empty frames. These frames will be filled with text if you add more text to the story, or if you increase the size of the story text.

- If there is still more text to go after filling the last frame, PagePlus stores it in an invisible **overflow area**, remembering that it's part of the story text. If you later add more frames or reduce the size of text in a frame, the rest of the story text is flowed in.

PagePlus keeps track of multiple linked frame sequences, and lets you flow several stories in the same publication. The **Text Manager** (accessed via the **Tools** menu) provides an overview of all stories and lets you choose which one you want to edit.

On text overflow, the frame's [icon] AutoFlow button can be used to create new frames for the overflowed story text. To control how the frame text is spread throughout available frames, you can use **AutoFit** to size story text automatically to the frame or use **Fit Text, Enlarge Text,** or **Shrink Text** for manual text sizing. See Fitting text to the frames on p. 118.

Fitting text to frames

Fitting story text precisely into a sequence of frames is part of the art of laying out publications.

⊞ ▣ If there's too much story text to fit in a frame sequence, PagePlus stores it in an invisible **overflow area** and the Link button on the last frame of the sequence displays a red square; an **AutoFlow** button appears next to the Link button. You might edit the story down or make more room for it by adding an extra frame or two to the sequence. Clicking the AutoFlow button adds additional frames and pages as needed (see below).

Once frames are in position it's still possible to control how text is distributed throughout the frame(s) via tools on the Frame context toolbar.

A ▾ The **Text Sizing** flyout offers three tools for controlling how frame text scales through the text frame. These are "one-off" operations (compared to the "continuous" **Autofit** options shown below).

A **Fit Text**
Click to scale the story's text size so it fits exactly into the available frame(s); further text added to the frame will cause text overflow. You can use this early on, to gauge how the story fits, or near the end, to apply the finishing touch. Fit Text first applies small point size changes, then small leading changes, then adjustments to the paragraph space below value, until the text fits.

A **Enlarge Text**
Click to increase the story's text size one increment (approx. 2%).

A **Shrink Text**
Click to reduce the story's text size one increment (approx. 2%).

Each frame's story text can adopt its own individual autofit setting as follows:

 The **AutoFit Options** flyout offers three autofit options which continuously act upon a selected frame's story text.

No AutoFit

This is the normal mode of operation where, if selected, text won't automatically scale throughout the selected text frame, possibly leaving partly empty frames at the end of the frame sequence.

Shrink Text on Overflow

If selected, extra text added to a selected frame will shrink all frame text to avoid text overflow.

AutoFit

If selected, the frame will always scale text automatically by adjusting text size (compare to **Fit Text** which fits text once, with any additional text causing text overflow).

AutoFlow

When importing text, it's a good idea to take advantage of the **AutoFlow** feature, which will automatically create text frames and pages until all the text has been imported. This way, enough frames are created to display the whole story. Then you can gauge just how much adjustment will be needed to fit the story to the available "real estate" in your publication.

If you add more text to a story while editing, or have reduced the size of frame, you may find that an overflow condition crops up. In this case you can decide whether to use AutoFit or click the frame's **AutoFlow** button.

To AutoFlow story text on the page:

- Click the **AutoFlow** button just to the left of the frame's **Link** button.

If no other empty frames are detected, you'll be prompted to autoflow text into a new frame(s) the same size as the original or to new frame(s) sized to the page. If an empty frame exists anywhere in your publication, PagePlus will flow text into that instead, before commencing with autoflow.

Linking text frames

When a text frame is selected, the frame includes a **Link** button at the bottom right which denotes the state of the frame and its story text. It also allows you to control how the frame's story flows to following frames:

 No Overflow
The frame is not linked to a following frame (it's either a standalone frame or the last frame in a sequence) and the frame is empty or the end of the story text is visible.

 Overflow
The populated frame is not linked (either standalone or last frame) and there is additional story text in the **hidden** overflow area.

An **Autoflow** button also appears to the left of the **Link** button.

 **Continued**
The frame is linked to a following frame. The end of the story text may be visible, or it may flow into the following frame.
Note: The button icon will be red if the final frame of the sequence is overflowing, or green if there's no overflow.

There are two basic ways to set up a linked sequence of frames:

- You can link a sequence of empty frames, then import the text.

- You can import the text into a single frame, then create and link additional frames into which the text automatically flows.

When frames are created by the AutoFlow option (for example when importing text), they are automatically linked in sequence.

To create a link or reorder the links between existing frames, you can use the **Link** button under the frame (or the controls on the Frame context toolbar). Remember to watch the cursor, which changes to indicate these operations.

- You can link to frames already containing text or are already in a link sequence.

- If the frame was not part of a link sequence, its text is merged into the selected text's story.

- Different frame sequences can be combined, creating unified story text.

To link the selected frame to an existing frame:

- Click the frame's **Link** button (showing or .)

- Click with the Textflow cursor on the frame to be linked to.

To link the selected frame to a newly drawn frame:

- As above, but instead of clicking a "target" frame, either click on the page (for a default frame) or drag across the page (to create a frame sized to your requirements). The latter is ideal for quickly mapping out linked frames across different pages.

To unlink the selected frame from the sequence:

- Click on **Continued**, then click with the Textflow cursor on the same frame.

Story text remains with the "old" frames. For example, if you detach the second frame of a three-frame sequence, the story text remains in the first and third frames, which are now linked into a two-frame story. The detached frame is always empty.

To navigate from frame to frame:

- Click in the text at the end of a text frame, then use your down arrow keyboard key to jump to the next frame.

Using artistic text

Artistic text is standalone text you type directly onto a page. Especially useful for headlines, pull quotes, and other special-purpose text, it's easily formatted with the standard text tools.

Here are some similarities between frame text and artistic text. Both text types let you:

- vary character and paragraph properties, apply named text styles, edit text in WritePlus and even import text.

- apply different line styles, fills (including gradient and bitmap fills), and transparency.

- access text via the Text Manager.

- track font usage with the Resource Manager.

- embed inline images.

- apply 2D/3D filter effects and rotate/flip.

- use proofing options such as AutoSpell/Spell Checker, Proof Reader, and Thesaurus.

And some differences...

- You can initially "draw" artistic text at a desired point size, and drag it to adjust the size later. Frame text reflows in its frame upon frame resize (but doesn't alter its text size).

- Artistic text can be applied to a path but frame text cannot.

- Artistic text won't automatically line wrap like frame text.

- Artistic text doesn't flow or link the way frame text does; the Frame context toolbar's text-fitting functions aren't applicable to artistic text.

To create artistic text:

1. Choose the  **Artistic Text Tool** from the **Tools** toolbar.

2. Set initial text properties (style, font, point size, etc.) as needed before typing, using the Text context toolbar.

3. Click on the page for an insertion point using a default point size, or drag the cross-hair cursor across the page to specify a particular size.

4. Type directly on the page to create the artistic text.

Once you've created an artistic text object, you can select, move, resize, delete, and copy it just as you would with a text frame. Solid colours, gradient/bitmap fills, and transparency can all be applied.

To resize or reproportion an artistic text object:

- To resize while maintaining the object's proportions, drag the resize handles.

- To resize freely, hold down the **Shift** key while dragging.

To edit artistic text:

- Drag to select a range of text, creating a blue selection.

You can also double-click to select a word, or triple-click to select all text.

Now you can type new text, apply character and paragraph formatting, edit the text in WritePlus, apply proofing options, and so on.

Putting text on a path

"Ordinary" straight-line artistic text is far from ordinary—but you can extend its creative possibilities even further by flowing it along a curved path.

The resulting object has all the properties of artistic text, plus its path is a Bézier curve that you can edit with the Pointer Tool as easily as any other line! In addition, text on a path is editable in some unique ways, as described below.

To apply a preset curved path to text:

1. Create an artistic text object.

2. With the text selected, on the Text context toolbar, click the down arrow on the **Path Text** flyout and choose a preset path.

The text now flows along the specified path, e.g. for "Path - Top Circle".

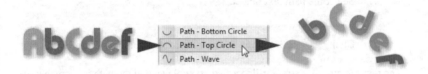

To add artistic text along an existing line or shape:

1. Create a freehand, straight, or curved line (see Drawing and editing lines on p. 201) or a shape (see Drawing and editing shapes on p. 204).

2. Choose the **A Artistic Text Tool** from the **Tools** toolbar.

3. Bring the cursor very close to the line. When the cursor changes to include a curve, click the mouse where you want the text to begin. Your line appears as a dashed path with an insertion point at its starting end.

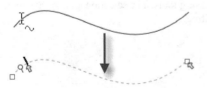

4. Begin typing at the insertion point. Text flows along the line, which has been converted to a path.

To fit existing text to an existing line or shape:

1. Create an artistic text object.

2. Create a freehand, straight, or curved line or a shape.

3. Select both objects. On the **Tools** menu, choose **Fit Text to Path**. The text now flows along the specified path.

To remove the text path:

1. Select the path text object.

2. Click ✗ **Path - None** on the Text context toolbar's Path flyout.

The text remains as a straight-line artistic text object and the path is permanently removed.

Editing text on the page

You can use the Pointer Tool to edit frame text, table text, or artistic text directly. On the page, you can select and enter text, set paragraph indents and tab stops, change text properties, apply text styles, and use Find and Replace. For editing longer stories, and for more advanced options, choose WritePlus (**Edit Story...** from the **Edit** menu).

Selecting and entering text

The selection of frame text, artistic text, and table text follows the conventions of the most up-to-date word-processing tools. The selection area is shaded in semi-transparent blue for clear editing.

> Nulla vestibulum eleifend
> nulla. Suspendisse potenti.
> Aliquam turpis nisi, venenatis
> non, accumsan nec, imperdiet
> laoreet, lacus.

Double-, triple- or quadruple-click selects a word, paragraph or all text, respectively. You can also make use of the **Ctrl**-click or drag for selection of non-adjacent words, the **Shift** key for ranges of text.

To edit text on the page:

1. Select the Pointer Tool, then click (or drag) in the text object. A standard insertion point appears at the click position (see below).
    - or -
    Select a single word, paragraph or portion of text.

2. Type to insert new text or overwrite selected text, respectively.

> Nulla vestibulum eleifend
> nulla. Suspendisse potenti.
> Aliquam turpis nisi, venenatis
> non, accumsan nec, imperdiet
> laoreet, lacus.

To start a new paragraph:

*   Press **Enter**.

To start a new line within the same paragraph (using a "line break" or "soft return"):

*   Press **Shift+Enter**.

The following two options apply only to frame text. You can use these shortcuts or choose the items from the **Insert>Break** submenu.

To flow text to the next column (Column Break), frame (Frame Break) or page (Page Break):

*   Press **Ctrl+Enter**, **Alt+Enter** or **Ctrl+Shift+Enter**, respectively.

To switch between insert mode and overwrite mode:

*   Press the **Insert** key.

To show special characters:

- Click the ¶ ▾ drop-down arrow on the **Hintline** toolbar, and select **Show Special Characters** (for paragraph marks and breaks; see below) or **Show Spaces** (Show Special Characters plus tabs, non-breaking spaces, hyphenation points, and "filled" normal spaces).

Praesent nisl tortor, laoreet eu,
dapibus quis, egestas non,
mauris.
 Cum sociis natoque penatibus,
nascetur ridiculus mus.

Nullam eleifend pharetra felis.
Mauris nibh velit, tristique
lacinia in.

Praesent nisl tortor, laoreet eu,
dapibus quis, egestas non,
mauris.↵
 Cum sociis natoque penatibus,
nascetur ridiculus mus.¶

Nullam eleifend pharetra felis.
Mauris nibh velit, tristique
lacinia in.§

Copying, pasting, and moving text

You can easily copy and paste text using standard commands; drag and drop of text is also supported.

If you don't place an insertion point on pasting, the text can be pasted into a new text frame directly.

Setting paragraph indents

When a text object is selected, markers on the horizontal ruler indicate the left indent, first line indent, and right indent of the current paragraph. You can adjust the markers to set paragraph indents, or use a dialog.

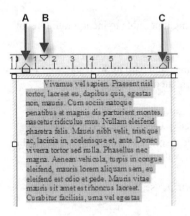

- The **Left** indent (**A**) is set in relation to the object's left margin (or text frame edge if margin not set).

- The **1st line** indent (**B**) is in relation to the left indent.

- The **Right** indent (**C**) is in relation to the object's right margin (or text frame edge if margin not set).

For details on setting frame margins, see Frame setup and layout (on p. 116).

To set the indents of the current paragraph:

- Drag the appropriate ruler marker(s) as shown above.
  - or -

- For quick left indents, select the **Increase Paragraph Indent** or **Decrease Paragraph Indent** button to increase or decrease indent, respectively. Indent is by the currently set default tab stop distance.
  - or -

- To adjust indent settings numerically, choose **Paragraph...** from the **Format** menu. In the Indentation box, you can enter values for Left, Right, 1st Line, or Hanging indents.

Working with Unicode text

PagePlus fully supports Unicode, making it possible to incorporate foreign characters or special symbols.

- To paste Unicode text from the Clipboard to the page, use **Edit>Paste Special...**, then select "Unformatted Unicode Text."

- Insert Unicode characters directly into your text by typing your Unicode Hex value and pressing **Alt+X**. The Alt+X keyboard operation toggles between the displayed character (e.g., @) and its Hex value (e.g., U+0040) equivalent.

- To export text in Unicode format, use WritePlus.

Using Find and Replace

You can search publication text for an extraordinary variety of items; not just words or parts of words, but a host of character and paragraph attributes such as fonts, styles, alignment, bullets and numbering, missing fonts, drop caps... even inline graphics and more! Once located, you can replace items either globally, or on a case-by-case basis.

To use Find and Replace on frame text:

1. Choose **Find & Replace...** from the **Edit** menu.

2. In the dialog, type the text to be found in the **Find** box and its replacement text (if any) in the **Replace** box. Click the down arrows to view recent items.

   Click either box's ⸢>⸣ button to use flyout menus to select formats or special characters, or define a regular expression (for a wildcard-type search).

3. Select the Range to be searched: **Current Story** (just the currently selected text object or story), or **All Stories** (all text), or **Current Selection** (only used with the Replace All function to operate on the currently selected text).

4. Select **Match whole word only** to match character sequences that have **white space** (space, tab character, page break, etc.) or punctuation at each end, or which are at the start/end of a paragraph. Select **Match case** for case-sensitive search. Select **Regular expressions** to treat the contents of the Find box as an expression, rather than as a literal string to be found.

5. Click **Find Next** to locate the next instance of the Find text after the insertion point.
    - or -
    Click **Find Previous** to locate the previous instance of the Find text.
    - or -
    Click **Select All** to highlight all instances of matching text in your document simultaneously.

6. Click **Replace** if you want to substitute with replacement text. Alternatively, click **Find Next** again to skip to the next matching text. Continue using the Replace option as required until you reach the end of your document.
    - or -
    Click **Replace All** to replace all instances of the found text with the replacement text at the same time. PagePlus reports when the search is completed.

7. Click **Close** to dismiss the Find and Replace dialog.

Setting text properties

PagePlus gives you a high degree of typographic control over characters and paragraphs, whether you're working with frame text, table text, or artistic text.

To apply basic text formatting:

1. Select the text.

2. Use buttons on the Text context toolbar to change text style, font, point size, attributes, paragraph alignment, bullets/numbering, or level.

To clear local formatting (restore plain/default text properties):

- Select a range of text with local formatting.

- Click on the **Clear Formatting** option on the Text context toolbar's text styles drop-down list (or Text Styles tab).

Using text styles

PagePlus lets you use named **text styles** (pre- or user-defined), which can be applied to frame text, table text, artistic text, index text or table of contents text. A text style is a set of character and/or paragraph attributes saved as a group. When you apply a style to text, you apply the whole group of attributes in just one step. For example, you could use named paragraph styles for particular layout elements, such as "Heading 1" or "Body", and character styles to convey meaning, such as "Emphasis", "Strong", or "Subtle Reference".

Styles can be applied to characters or paragraphs using either the Text context toolbar or the Text Styles tab. Both paragraph and character styles can be managed from the **Text Style Palette**.

Paragraph and character styles

A **paragraph style** is a complete specification for the appearance of a paragraph, including all font and paragraph format attributes. Every paragraph in PagePlus has a paragraph style associated with it.

- PagePlus includes a built-in **default** paragraph style called **"Normal"** which is left-aligned, 12pt Times New Roman. When you create frame text from scratch you'll be using the **Body** text style based on Normal; artistic text uses **Artistic Body** text style, based on the Body style. This hierarchical approach makes for powerful text style control.

- Applying a paragraph style to text updates all the text in the paragraph except sections that have been locally formatted. For example, a single word marked as bold would remain bold when the paragraph style was updated or changed.

A **character style** includes only font attributes (name, point size, bold, italic, etc.), and you apply it at the character level—that is, to a range of selected characters—rather than to the whole paragraph.

- Typically, a character style applies emphasis (such as italics, bolding or colour) to whatever underlying font the text already uses; the assumption is that you want to keep that underlying font the same. The base character style is shown in the Text Styles tab (or palette) as **"Default Paragraph Font,"** which has no specified attributes but basically means "whatever font the paragraph style already uses."

- Applying the Default Paragraph Font option from the Text Styles tab (or the Text context toolbar's Styles box) will strip any selected local character formatting you've added and will restores original text attributes (paragraph styles are not affected).

- As with paragraph styles, you can define any number of new character styles using different names and attributes (or adopt a pre-defined character style).

Text style hierarchies

All paragraph or character text styles available in PagePlus are ultimately based on the respective Normal and Default Paragraph Font text styles.

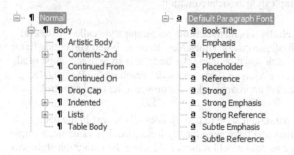

Paragraph styles   Character styles

So why have this hierarchy of text styles? The key reason for this is the ability to change a text style at any "level" in the hierarchy in order to affect all "child" styles which belong to it.

Working with named styles

Body ▾   The named style of the currently selected text is displayed in either the Text Styles tab or the **Styles** drop-down list on the Text context toolbar. A character style (if one is applied locally) may be shown; otherwise it indicates the paragraph style.

To apply a named style:

1. Using the Pointer Tool, click in a paragraph (if applying a paragraph style) or select a range of text (if applying a character style).

2. Display the **Text Styles** tab and select a style from the style list.
   - or -
   On the Text context toolbar, click the arrow to expand the Styles drop-down list and select a style name.

The Text Style tab highlights the paragraph or character style applied to any selected text.

As both paragraph and character formatting can be applied to the same text, all of the current text's formatting is displayed in the **Current format** box on the tab. In the example below, currently selected text has a Strong character style applied over a Normal paragraph style.

Current format: Body + Strong

To update a named style using the properties of existing text:

1. Make your desired formatting changes to any text that uses a named style.

2. On the **Text Styles** tab, right-click the style and choose **Update <style> to Match Selection**.

All text using the named style, throughout the publication, takes on the new properties.

To create a new paragraph or character style:

Either:

1. On the **Text Styles** tab, select the paragraph or character style on which you want your new style to be based.

2. Click **Create Paragraph Style** or **Create Character Style**.

- or -

- Choose **Text Style Palette...** in the **Format** menu, and with a "base" style selected in the dialog, click the **Create...** button.

Then:

3. In the **Text Style** dialog, define the style **Name**, the style to be **Based on**, **Style for the following paragraph**, and the style to be changed to if Increase Level is applied. Check **Always list in Studio** to ensure the style will always appear in the **Text Styles** tab.

4. In the left tree menu change any character or paragraph attributes, tabs, bullets, and drop caps you want to include in the new style definition.

5. Click **OK** to create the style, or **Cancel** to abandon changes.

To create a new style using the properties of existing text:

1. Format the text as desired.

2. To define a character style, select a range of reformatted text. To define a paragraph style, deselect text but leave a blinking cursor (insertion point) within the newly formatted section.

3. Type a new style name into the Text context toolbar's **Styles** drop-down list and press **Enter**.

The new style is defined with the properties of the selected text.

To modify an existing style:

From the Text Styles tab:

1. Right-click on the character or paragraph style you want to modify and then choose **Modify <style>...**
   - or -

   With a style selected, select ▨ **Manage** from the **Text Styles** tab, then choose the **Modify...** button.

2. From the Text Style dialog, define (or change) the style name, base style, and any character or paragraph attributes, tabs, bullets, and drop caps you want to include in the style definition.

3. Click **OK** to accept style properties, or **Cancel** to abandon changes.

4. Click **Apply** to update text, or click **Close** to maintain the style in the publication for future use.

Alternatively, choose **Text Style Palette...** from the **Format** menu to modify styles and to change text defaults (see p. 106).

To delete one or more text styles:

- Right-click a text style and select **Delete <style>**....

- From the dialog, click **Remove**. For deletion of multiple styles, check multiple style names first. For removal of all or unused styles, use appropriate buttons.

⚠ Take care when deleting styles. Styles based on a checked "parent" style will be checked for deletion.

Removing local formatting

✎ ▾ To return characters and/or paragraphs back to their original formatting, click on **Clear Formatting** in the Text Styles tab. This is great for reverting some formatting which hasn't quite worked out! You can clear the formatting of selected characters, paragraphs, or both depending on what text is currently selected. The following table indicates the effects of different types of text selection on clear formatting.

Selection	Clicking Clear Formatting affects..
Word	Character
Range of text	Character
Single paragraph	Character and Paragraph
Multiple paragraphs	Paragraph
Story text	Character and Paragraph
Text frame	Character and Paragraph

✎ ▾
∂ Clear Character Formatting
¶ Clear Paragraph Formatting
⁄ Clear All Formatting

You also have the flexibility to be more explicit about how clear formatting is applied by clicking on the Clear Formatting option's drop-down arrow.

To remove local formatting:

1. Select locally formatted characters or paragraph(s) as described in the above table.

2. Either:

   - Select **Clear Formatting** from the **Styles** drop-down list on the Text context toolbar.
     - or -

   - On the **Text Styles** tab, you can:

   - Click ⬚ ▾ **Clear All Formatting** from the drop-down list (or **Clear Text Formatting** from the **Format** menu).
     - or -

   - Select **Clear Character Formatting** from the drop-down list to remove all local character formatting (leaving paragraph formatting untouched).
     - or -

   - Select **Clear Paragraph Formatting** from the drop-down list to remove all local paragraph formatting (leaving character formatting untouched).

Like **Clear Formatting**, you can use ⬚ ▾ **Reapply Styles** on the **Text Styles** tab (or Text context toolbar) to clear all local overrides leaving the default text. However, where Clear Formatting reverts the text to Normal style, Reapply styles reverts the text back to its current name style. Use **Reapply Character Style** (retaining paragraph styles overrides), **Reapply Paragraph Style** (retaining character style overrides), and **Reapply Both Styles** to remove both character or paragraph style overrides simultaneously.

⬚ If you prefer, you can remove a style's formatting, enabling you to start building up your text style again. Choose **Manage** on the Text Styles tab, click the **Modify** button, then click the **Clear All** button from the General section.

Changing common styles

Changing one character or paragraph style for another is very simple for a single portion of text. However, in PagePlus, it's just as easy to swap one style for another by selecting multiple instances of the style and choosing an alternative style. This swaps styles across paragraphs and throughout entire stories all at the same time.

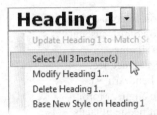

To select (and change) a style throughout your document:

1. Right-click a style displayed on the **Text Styles** tab.

2. If the style is used in your document, you'll see a "*Select All n instance(s)*" message (*n* is the number of times the style is used).

    If there are no occurrences of the style, you'll see a "*Not currently used*" message.

3. Click the message label—text formatted with the chosen style is highlighted.

4. Hover over style names in your styles list, then click on a chosen style to apply the style to the selected text.

Wrapping text

PagePlus lets you wrap frame text around the contours of a separate object. Usually, this means wrapping text to a picture that overlaps or sits above a text frame. But you can wrap frame text around a picture, shape, artistic text, table, or another frame. Wrapping is accomplished by changing the **wrap setting** for the object to which text will wrap.

> Vestibulum semper enim non eros. Sed vitae arcu. Aliquam erat volutpat. Praesent odio nisl, suscipit at, rhoncus sit amet, porttitor sit amet, leo. Aenean hendrerit est. Etiam ac augue. Morbi tincidunt neque ut lacus. Duis vulputate cursus orci. Mauris justo lorem, scelerisque sit amet, placerat sed, condimentum in, leo. Donec urna est, semper quis, auctor eget, ultrices in, purus. Etiam rutrum.

To wrap text around an object:

1. Select the object around which you want the text to wrap.

2. Click the ▣ **Wrap Settings** button on the **Arrange** toolbar.

   - Select the manner in which text will wrap around the object by clicking a sample, i.e.

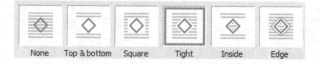

| None | Top & bottom | Square | Tight | Inside | Edge |

- Choose which side(s) the chosen wrapping method will be applied, again by clicking a sample.

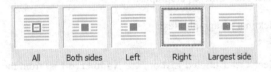

| All | Both sides | Left | Right | Largest side |

The examples show tight wrapping applied to the right of the object only.

3. Click **OK**.

In addition, you can specify the **Distance from text**: the "standoff" between the object's **wrap outline** and adjacent text. (The wrap outline is a contour that defines the object's edges for text wrapping purposes.) Different object types have different initial wrap outlines. For QuickShapes, the wrap outline corresponds exactly to the object's edges, while for closed shapes the outline is a rectangle.

You can manually adjust the wrap outline using the Curve context toolbar for more precise text fitting. See PagePlus Help for more information.

Creating a bulleted or numbered list

You can turn a series of paragraphs into **bulleted**, **numbered** or **multi-level lists**. Bullets are especially useful when listing items of interest in no specific order of preference, numbered lists for presenting step-by-step procedures (by number or letter), and multi-level lists for more intelligent hierarchical lists with prefixed numbers, symbols, or a mix of both, all with supporting optional text (see Using multi-level lists on p. 143).

Bulleted list *Numbered list* *Multi-level list*

Lists can be applied to normal text (as local formatting) or to text styles equally.

To create a simple bulleted or numbered list:

1. Select one or more paragraphs.
   - or -
   Click in a paragraph's text.

2. Select ▤ **Bulleted List** or ▤ **Numbered List** from the Text context toolbar.

The list style used is the first preset shown in the Text Style dialog described below.

To create a bulleted or numbered list (using presets):

1. Select one or more paragraphs.
   - or -
   Click in a paragraph's text.

2. Select **Bullets and Numbering...** from the **Format** menu.

3. From the Text Style dialog's Bullets and Numbering menu option, choose **Bullet**, **Number**, or **Multi-Level** from the **Style** drop-down list.

4. Select one of the preset formats shown by default.
   - or -
   For a custom list, click the **Details** button to display, then alter custom options.

5. Click **OK** to apply list formatting.

For number and multi-level lists, check **Restart numbering** to restart numbering from the current cursor position in the list; otherwise, leave the option unchecked.

▤ ▤ Turn off list formatting by clicking the Text context toolbar's buttons again.

Using multi-level lists

For multi-level lists, as opposed to bulleted and numbered lists, you can set a different character (symbol, text or number) to display at each level of your list. Levels are normally considered to be subordinate to each other, where Level 1 (first level), Level 2 (second), Level 3 (third), etc. are of decreasing importance in the list. For example, the following simple multi-level numbered passage of text is arranged at three levels.

The flexibility of PagePlus's multi-level bullet and numbering system means that you have full control over what gets displayed at each level. For this reason, no common numbering schema needs to exist between levels, i.e. the list could equally be prefixed with a different symbol, text prefix, or number combination at each level.

If you apply a multi-level preset to a range of text you'll get a list with the preset's Level 1 format applied by default. Unless you use text styles, you'll have to change to levels 2, 3, 4, etc. to set the correct level for your list entry.

1 Vestibulum velit orci, Nullam sed enim. Dui
  1.1 Lorem ipsum pendisse poten
  1.2 Mauris vitae a nean arcu elit, ligula.
   1.2.1 Quisqu
   1.2.2 Donec Duis b molest tum le

2 In hac habitasse plate Proin mattis eleifend

3 Proin mattis eleifend pede tellus, dictum eg

Changing list levels on selected paragraphs:

- Click the   **Increase Paragraph Indent** or   **Decrease Paragraph Indent** button on the Text context toolbar to increment or decrement the current level by one.

The multi-level presets offer some simple but commonly used schemas for paragraph list formatting. However, if you want to create your own lists or modify an existing list (your own or a preset), use the **Details** button in the Text Style dialog when Multi-Level style is selected. See PagePlus Help for more details.

Assigning bullets, numbers, and levels to styles

PagePlus lets you easily associate any bulleted, numbered or multi-level list style (either preset or custom list) to an existing text style. See Using text styles on p. 132.

Inserting cross-references

PagePlus allows you to cross-reference to headings and anchored text, tables, pictures, or diagrams throughout your publication. Numbered paragraphs, footnotes/endnotes, and next/previous frames can also be cross-referenced.

By choosing the "target" of the cross-reference, i.e. what the reference is to (e.g., a heading or anchor), you can then choose how the cross-reference will appear, typically as a page number or item name. This can also appear as the text "above" or "below", a text number, or referenced header/content.

To insert a cross-reference field:

1. (Optional) In advance, create anchors to any objects you'd like to cross-reference to.

2. Click in the text for an insertion point (or make a text selection).

3. From the Insert menu, select **Information>Cross-reference...**

4. From the dialog, choose a target that you want to reference to from the **Type** drop-down list. Types include:

    - **Anchor**: a named anchor, which may be attached to an object or text via **Insert>Anchor....**

    - **Bookmark**: a named bookmark as assigned with **Insert>PDF Bookmarks....**

    - **Heading**: a paragraph of text formatted with a heading text style (e.g. Heading 1).

    - **Numbered paragraph**: text formatted as a numbered list or numbered heading.

    - **Footnote or endnote**: the first paragraph of a footnote or an endnote.

    - **Next frame/Previous frame**: when text flows through a series of linked frames you can reference the subsequent text frame into which the current frame's text will next flow. Previous does the reverse—you reference the previous text frame from which the flowing text has comes from.

5. In the **Item** list, which changes with the Type selected, select the item of that type in your publication. These can be sorted alphabetically or by page number, by clicking on the appropriate column.

6. The **Insert as** section lets you choose how the reference will appear. You can pick from one of several choices of target.

    - **Page number**: the number of the page the target is on.

    - **Above/below**: the position of the target relative to the cross-reference. This may also display as "left" or "right" if the target is on the same page, or "opposite" in a publication with facing pages.

    - **Item name**: For anchors and bookmarks only, the name is taken from the target's Name shown in the previous Item list.

    - The remaining options only make sense when the target is text:

- **Text number**: the number of the numbered list, heading, footnote or paragraph. When the target is deep in a multi-level numbered list, like "1.B.iii.", you can pick:

- (no context): just the target's own number, e.g. "iii.".

- (relative context): which list levels are included depends on whether the cross-reference is in part of the same list as the target. For example, if the cross-reference is in "1.C.ii." (a later part of the same top-level list), then the reference would appear as "B.iii".

- (full context): include numbers from all levels of the list, e.g. "1.B.iii.".

  For a normal paragraph (not in a numbered list or footnote), its number is the count from its most recent heading, and the full context includes the text of that heading. For example, "Details/3" would refer to the 3rd paragraph since the "Details" heading.

- **Referenced header**: the text of the most recent header of the target. Use this for referencing heading text.

- **Referenced content**: the actual text of the target paragraph. You can limit the number of words to be included with the **Up to** input box; set this to a large number to get the entire paragraph.

7. **Prefix/Suffix**: Use to add text before and after the reference. For example, you could surround a reference with brackets or quotes, or include "p. " as a prefix to a page number reference.

8. **Number separator**. Often numbered lists include their own separators and punctuation, for example "(A)". This check box discards the original separator and replaces it with the given new one, entered into the adjacent box. This is especially useful with multi-level lists with context, where "1.(A)1." can be reformatted by the cross-reference as, for example, "1.A.1".

9. Keep **Insert as Hyperlink** checked to make the cross-reference a hyperlink; this is ideal for electronic publishing to PDF or HTML. For printing to desktop printers, uncheck the option if needed.

10. Click **OK**.

To edit a cross-reference:

- Right-click the cross-reference field and select **Edit Cross-reference**.

To jump to a cross-referenced target:

- Right-click the cross-reference field and select **Goto Target**.

Continued From/Continued On cross-references

For easy story navigation between linked text frames, PagePlus provides "**Continued From/Continued On**" cross-references. When enabled, these appear at the top and bottom of your text frame, respectively, to indicate where the story text continues, i.e. to the previous or next text frame on the same or different publication page.

viverra malesuada, enim

. Cras risus turpis, varius
onummy felis. Etiam
cipit erat, nec suscipit sem

*(Continued on **page 2**)*

Like other cross-references, these references will automatically update if frames are moved to a different page or new pages are added.

To insert a "Continued From/On" cross-reference:

1. Select the text frame which is linked to another frame you want to reference to.

2. From the **Insert** menu, select **Information>Continued From** or **Continued On**. The cross-reference appears at the top or bottom of the text frame, respectively.

By default, you'll create a page number cross-reference. However you can change the cross-reference to a different Type by right-clicking the field and selecting **Edit Cross-reference**.

Inserting user details

When you create a publication from a design template for the first time, you may be prompted to update your user details (Name, Company, Telephone number, etc.) in a User Details dialog. These details will automatically populate pre-defined text "fields" in your publication, making it personalized.

PagePlus supports business sets (i.e., stored sets of user details) which can be created per customer and applied to your publication. This lets you create publication variants, with each differing just in their user details. You can choose which set to use when you start with a new design template (or at any time during your session).

You can also use this User Details dialog to review and update user details at any time, as well as define global and publication variables for use in all PagePlus publications or just the current publication.

To add, edit or change user details:

1. Click the User Details button on the Pages context toolbar (deselect objects to view).

2. Enter new information into the spaces on the **Business Sets** or **Home** tab (a **Calendars** tab will appear if there is a calendar in your publication).

3. Click **Update**.

If you're starting from scratch, you need to have user details fields placed in your publication.

Inserting your own fields

You can also insert one or more User Details fields into any publication at any time.

To insert a User Detail field:

1. Select the Pointer Tool and click in the text for an insertion point.

2. From the **Insert** menu, select **Information>User Details...**.

3. Select a user detail entry and optionally any text **Prefix** or **Suffix** to include with your user details, e.g. *(Home) Name*.

4. Click **OK**.

For existing publications, the fields (once edited) can be updated or swapped at the click of a button.

> If inserting business user details, the details from the currently active business set are used.
>
> Hyperlinks and cross-references can be added to fields. For more information, see Hyperlinking an object (p. 177) and Inserting cross-references (p. 144).

To update user details:

*   Enter new information in the User Details dialog (via **Tools>Set User Details...**).

*   Click the **Update** button to automatically update any altered field currently placed in your publication. This field will remain linked to User Details until it is deleted.

To swap user detail fields:

1. Select the user detail field you want to swap out.

2. Click **Edit Field** on the control bar above the selected field.

3.   In the dialog, select an entry to insert, e.g. *(Home) Name,* and optionally any text **Prefix** or **Suffix** to include with your user details.

4.   Click **OK**.

Converting fields to text

You can convert your user detail fields to text to edit in your publication. Once converted, the user details will no longer function as fields but instead, as plain text.

1.   Select the user detail field want to convert.

2.   Click **Convert Field to Text** on the control bar above the selected field.

Creating business sets

If you are designing publications for more than one customer, you can store and assign different sets of business user details for each. Think of a business set as a profile, storing a unique set of user details under a chosen name.

To create a business set:

1.   From the User Details dialog (Business Sets tab), click **New....**

2.   Enter a new name for the business set and click **OK**. Your new set becomes active as shown in the **Select Set** drop-down list.

3.   Enter information in the User Details dialog, then click **Update**.

Once you've created a business set and applied it to your publication, the settings will be stored with the publication.

Business sets allow you to store different user details for each publication you create.

To swap to a different business set:

*   Select an alternative set from the **Select Set** drop-down list, then click **Update**.

To rename or delete a business set:

1.   Choose the business set from the **Select Set** drop-down list.

2.   Select **Rename** or **Delete**.

Inserting variables

If you have some repeating text used throughout your publication which you'd like to swap for replacement text, you can use **variables**. Typically, you would do this to change a product name or version, making your publication easy to update when product versions change. The variable fields change automatically, updating with the new values.

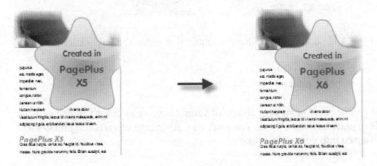

Variables are used in a similar way to user details (see p. 148). They can be added and inserted just like user detail fields and be updated from the same User Details dialog.

The variable can be stored just within the publication or made globally for other publications. The latter would be a good choice for product names as they are likely to be used again globally in a company environment.

To add, edit or delete variables:

1.   Click **User Details** on the Pages context toolbar (deselect objects to view).

2.   Select the **Global** or **Publication** tab if you want the added variable to be available to all publications or just to the document, respectively.

3. From either tab, click the **Add** button.

4. In the variables list, type over the created **Variable** name, giving it a unique string that identifies the variable easily.

Variable	Value
Product_Name_Version	

5. Click in the column adjacent to the new Variable and type the variable value (i.e. the text that will appear on the page).

Variable	Value
Product_Name_Version	PagePlus X6

6. Add additional variables as required to either the Publication or Global tab.

7. Click **Update**.

Once you've decided on your choice of variables you can insert variables as fields in place of "static" text. You can't take advantage of variables unless they are inserted into your publication.

To insert a variable field:

1. Click in the text for an insertion point (or make a text selection).

2. From the **Insert** menu, select **Information>Variable...** from the submenu.

3. From the dialog's drop-down list, select your variable from where you stored it in User Details (i.e., Global or Publication).

4. Select a variable entry and optionally any text **Prefix** or **Suffix** to include with your variable.

5. Click **OK**.

To display variable fields in your text:

- From the **View** menu's **Special Characters** flyout, check **Variables**.

When you want to change a variable, all that's needed is to edit and update the variable's value. The variable fields throughout your publication are updated with the new values.

To update variables:

1. Click User Details on the Pages context toolbar (deselect objects to view).

2. Edit the existing variables with new values.

Variable	Value
Product_Name_Version	PagePlus X7

3. Click **Update**.

You can swap variable fields and convert fields to text in the same way as with user details (see p. 148).

You can also add hyperlinks and cross-references to variable fields. For more information, see Hyperlinking an object (p. 177) and Inserting cross-references (p. 144).

If you come across some text (either artistic, frame, or table) that you'd like to be made into a variable, it can be converted to a variable easily.

To convert text to a variable:

1. Select the text.

2. Right-click the text, and select **Create variable from text**.

3. From the dialog, choose to make the variable available in the publication or globally in the Type drop-down list.

4. Enter a **Name** and **Value** pair, and a prefix/suffix if needed.

5. Click **OK**.

Using Auto-Correct and Spell as you Type

PagePlus includes two powerful support tools to nip possible spelling errors in the bud. The **Auto-Correct** feature overcomes common typing errors and lets you build a custom list of letter combinations and substitutions to be applied automatically as you type. You can also **underline spelling mistakes as you type** to mark possible problem words in your story text with red underline. Both features apply to frame text, table text, and artistic text.

If you prefer to address spelling issues in larger doses at the same time, you can run the Spell Checker anytime.

Auto-Correct

To set options for automatic text correction:

1. Choose **Options...** from the **Tools** menu and select the **Text>Auto-Correct>Options** page.

2. Check your desired Auto-Correct options.

For any checked options, auto-correction will be enabled. Additionally, a pre-defined correction list for automatic text replacement can be used; the list, populated by commonly typed misspellings and their correct equivalents, can also be added to for custom corrections.

To use a correction list:

1. Choose **Options...** from the **Tools** menu and select the **Text>Auto-Correct>Replacements** page.

2. Select a language from the **Language** drop-down list.

3. Check **Replace text while typing** to turn on Auto-Correct. The pre-defined text replacements will be applied when you type the misspelt words.

☑ Replace text while typing	
Replace:	With:
	dfwsvssvcsd

1/2	½
1/4	¼
3/4	¾
abotu	about
abouta	about a
aboutit	about it
abscence	absence
accesories	accessories
accidant	accident

To add custom misspellings to the correction list:

1. In the **Replace** field, type a name for the Auto-Correct entry. This is the abbreviation or word to be replaced automatically as you type. For example, if you frequently mistype "product" as "prodcut," type "prodcut" in the Replace box.

2. In the **With** field, type the text to be automatically inserted in place of the abbreviation or word in the **Replace** field.

3. Click the **Add** button to add the new entry to the list.

4. To modify an entry in the correction list, select it in the list, then edit it in the **Replace** and **With** field above. Click the **Replace** button below.

5. To remove an entry, select it and click **Delete**.

PagePlus also provides a pre-defined abbreviations dictionary which is used to prevent inadvertent capitalization of abbreviations. You can add your own abbreviations to the dictionary via **Tools>Options...** (Text>Auto-Correct>Abbreviations).

Spell as you Type

Use this feature to firstly indicate possible problem words in your text using red underline, and secondly to offer (via right-click) a range of alternative correct spellings to replace the problem words.

To check spelling as you type:

- Ensure the **Underline spelling mistakes as you type** feature is turned on (from **Tools>Options>Text>Proofreading**).

In your document, words with spelling problems are indicated with a red squiggly underline. You can review these by eye, with the option of replacing the words with suggested alternatives.

- To replace a marked word, place an insertion point in a marked word then right-click to choose an alternative spelling from the context menu.

- To tell PagePlus to ignore (leave unmarked) all instances of the marked word in the publication, choose **Ignore All** (or just **Ignore** for this instance only).

- To add the marked word (as spelled) to your personal dictionary, choose **Add to Dictionary** from the right-click menu. This means PagePlus will subsequently ignore the word in any publication.

- Select **Check Spelling** to run the Spell Checker.

Spell-checking

The **Spell Checker** lets you check the spelling of text in your current story, all stories on the current page, or all stories in your publication. You can customize the built-in dictionary by adding your own words.

To help trap typographic errors and fix spelling problems while creating text, use Auto-Correct and Check spelling as you type, respectively.

Multilingual spell checking is supported by use of up to 14 dictionaries. Any language can be enabled globally from **Tools>Options>Text>Proofreading** or applied specifically to text or paragraphs via the Language Selector in the Character tab. Spell checking can be turned off temporarily by selecting "None" as a language type—this could be useful when working with text containing lots of unusual terms (perhaps scientific or proprietary terminology).

To check spelling:

1. (Optional) To check a single story, first make sure the text or frame is selected.

2. Choose **Spell Checker...** from the **Tools** menu.

3. (Optional) In the dialog, click **Options...** to set preferences for ignoring words in certain categories, such as words containing numbers, domain names, or with specific capitalizations.

4. Select **Check currently selected story only**, **Check all stories on the current page**, or **Check all stories in my publication** to select the scope of the search.

5. Click **Start** to begin the spelling check.

When a problem is found, PagePlus highlights the problem word. The dialog offers alternative suggestions, and you can choose to **Change** or **Ignore** this instance (or all instances) of the problem word, with the option of clicking **Add** to add the problem word to your dictionary.

6. Spell checking continues until you click the **Close** button or the spell-check is completed.

Automatic proofreading

The **Proof Reader** checks for grammar and readability errors in text in your publication. You can use Proof Reader from either PagePlus or WritePlus.

To start automatic proofreading:

1. To check a single story, first make sure the text or text object is selected.

2. Choose **Proof Reader...** from the **Tools** menu.

3. If necessary, click the **Options** button to set options for proofreading, including a spell-check option and the level of formality (with checks for rule types).

4. Select options to **Check currently selected story only**, **Check all stories on the current page**, or **Check all stories in my publication** to select the scope of the search.

5. Click **Start** to begin proof reading.

When a problem is found, PagePlus highlights the problem. The dialog offers alternative suggestions, and you can choose to **Change** or **Ignore** this instance (or all instances) of the problem.

6. Proofreading continues until you click the **Close** button or the process is completed.

Creating text-based tables

Tables are ideal for presenting text and data in a variety of easily customizable row-and-column formats, with built-in spreadsheet capabilities.

			£/€
Ranunculus aquatilis	345-56	1	4.24/4.97
Myosotis scorpiodes	334-B299	2	4.64/5.44
Nymphoides peltata	089-78	2	2.93/3.44
Menyanthes trifoliate	455-01	1	7.10/8.32
Caltha palustris	345-33	1	2.55/2.99

Each cell in a table behaves like a mini-frame. Like frame text you can vary character and paragraph properties, apply named text styles, apply photo-based borders, embed inline images, apply text colour fills (solid, gradient, or bitmap), track font usage with the Resource Manager, and use proofing options such as Spell Checker, Proof Reader, and Thesaurus. Some unique features include number formatting and formula insertion.

Rather than starting from scratch, PagePlus is supplied with a selection of pre-defined table formats, i.e. templates, that can be used. Simply pick one and fill in the cells with content.

PagePlus lets you:

- Edit the pre-defined format before adding a new table to the page.

- Create your own custom formats without creating a table. See Creating custom table formats in PagePlus Help.

- Edit existing tables to fit a different format (pre-defined or custom).

To create a table:

1. On the **Tools** toolbar, choose the **Table Tool** from the **Table** flyout.

2. Click on the page or pasteboard, or drag to set the table's dimensions. The **Create Table** dialog opens with a selection of preset table formats shown in the **Format** window.

3. Step through the list to preview the layouts and select one. To begin with a plain table, select (**Default**).

4. (Optional) Click **Edit** if you want to further customize your chosen format.

5. Set the **Table Size**. This is the number of rows and columns that make up the table layout.

6. Click **OK**. The new table appears on the page.

Plan your table layout in advance, considering the number of rows/columns needed!

Inserting a calendar

The **Calendar Wizard** helps you design month-at-a-glance calendars for use in your publication.

January 2012

1	S
2	M
3	T
4	W
5	T
6	F
7	S
8	S
9	M

The calendar is created as a scalable text-based table so you can edit text using the standard text tools. The properties of a selected calendar are similar to those of a table, and can be modified identically (see PagePlus Help). Like custom table formats you can create your own custom calendar formats.

The wizard lets you set up the month/year and calendar style/format, and controls the inclusion of personal events and/or public holidays. The **Calendar Event Manager** lets you add personal events before or after adding a calendar to the page.

For calendar-specific properties, a context toolbar lets you change an existing calendar's month/year, modify calendar-specific properties, and manage calendar events (both personal and public holidays).

When you have one or more calendars in your document, you can, at any time, update all their details in one go via **User Details**—in the same way that you'd set up the date (along with the time) on some alarm clocks. This is especially useful if you want to update the year on a year-to-view page, composed of 12 monthly calendars—you only need to change the year in one place.

> If you have adopted a calendar-based design template, you'll be initially prompted to configure **global** calendar details via the User Details dialog. This updates all calendar details throughout your PagePlus document.

To insert a calendar:

1. Click the Table flyout on the **Tools** toolbar and choose ▦ **Insert Calendar**.

2. Click again on your page, or drag out to set the desired size of the calendar.

3. From the displayed **Calendar Wizard**, define options for your calendar including setting the year and month, calendar style (square, or in single or double column format), week start day, room to write, display options, switching on personal events/holidays, and calendar format.

   To have your country's public holidays shown, check **Add public holidays** in the wizard and select a **Region** from the associated drop-down list. To add personal events, check **Add personal events** additionally.

4. Click **Finish** to complete the wizard.

If you plan to use your calendar in subsequent years, simply update the **Year** setting in **Tools>Set User Details**.

To view and edit a selected calendar's properties:

1. Click ▦ **Edit Calendar** on the Calendar context toolbar.

2. Choose an appropriate tab and make your modification, then press **OK**.

Right-click on a row/column header within the calendar to select, insert, delete, and adjust widths/heights for rows (or columns), as well as autofit to cell contents, but take care not to corrupt your table formatting!

Adding public holidays

When you create a calendar you can set up the appropriate public holidays for the country you reside in. The holidays will show up in your calendar automatically if **Add public holidays** is checked in Calendar Properties.

To enable public holidays:

1. Select your calendar's bounding box, and click 🗓 **Edit Calendar** on the context toolbar.

2. From the Events tab, check **Add public holidays**.

3. (Optional) Swap to a different country's public holiday settings by using the **Region** drop-down list.

4. Click **OK**.

To display public holidays:

1. Select your calendar's bounding box.

2. Click 🗓 **Calendar Events** on the context toolbar.

3. Enable the **Show public holidays** option.

Adding personal events

You can complement your public holiday listings (e.g., Easter holidays) by adding personal events such as birthdays, anniversaries, and bill payments (unfortunately!) so that the events show up on your calendar—simply use the **Calendar Events** button on a selected calendar's context toolbar. Events show automatically on your calendar under the chosen date.

To enable personal events:

1. Select your calendar's bounding box, and click 🗓 **Edit Calendar** on the context toolbar.

2. From the Events tab, check **Add personal events**.

3. Click **OK**.

To add an event:

1. Select your calendar's bounding box.

2. Click ![] **Calendar Events** on the context toolbar.

3. (Optional) Select **Show events by date** to view your events in a more traditional calendar layout.

4. Click ![] **New event**.

5. ![] From the dialog, type, use the up/down arrows, or click the **Browse** button to select a date.

6. Enter your event text into the text input box. This displays in your calendar under the chosen date.

7. If the event is a birthday or other annual event, check **Event recurs annually**.

8. Click **OK**. The event appears in the event list under the chosen date.

9. When you have finished adding events, click **Save**.

> Use the ![] **Edit event** or ✕ **Delete event** buttons to modify or delete an existing event.

Inserting database tables

As a great way of producing a database report in your publication, it is possible for a database table to be imported and presented as a PagePlus table. The database table could be from one of a comprehensive range of database file formats (Serif databases (*.sdb), Microsoft Access, dBASE), as well as from HTML files, Excel files, ODBC, and various delimited text files.

For multi-table databases, PagePlus lets you select the table to be inserted.

For a high degree of control, it is also possible to filter and sort your database records prior to import.

> Insertion of database tables adopts the same principles as those used for Mail merge (see p. 180). However, instead of creating letters or labels you are merging content into a table.

To insert a database table:

1. Click ⊞ **Insert Database table** from the **Tools** toolbar's Table flyout.

2. Using the pointer, draw an area on your page that will contain your database information.

> If there are many fields in your database table you may consider presenting the information on a page with landscape orientation. Alternatively, you can choose only a subset of those fields.

3. In the dialog, navigate to your database file and select it. Use the drop-down list to change file format if you can't find the database file you require.

4. Click **Open**.

5. (Optional; for multi-table databases) The **Select Table** dialog displays the tables within your database. Select your table and click **OK**.

6. The **Merge List** dialog shows all the table rows (records) in the table—choose to **Select All** records, **Toggle Select** (invert all current selections) or use a custom **Filter...** The filter option also lets you sort the records to be merged. The **Edit...** button lets you edit Serif Database SDB files only. Click **OK**.

7. The list of fields available in the table are shown in the **Select Fields** dialog. Uncheck any fields that you don't want to be included in the import process. Again, Select All, Select None, or Toggle Select options are available.

8. Click the **OK** button. The database table appears on your page.

Filtering your records

Records can be filtered via the Merge List's **Filter...** button by using the Filter Records tab then subsequently sorted into any combination with the accompanying Sort Records tab. The option helps you limit the number of records imported to only those you require.

You can use the Boolean operators "And" and "Or" to build up your filter criteria row-by-row.

The Sort Records tab is used to sort by three prioritized field names, either in ascending or descending order.

Creating tables of contents

Publications with many pages benefit greatly from a Table of Contents (TOC), whether electronic or printed. These not only provide a useful overview of your publication's content, but are also vital for page navigation (by eye or hyperlink).

In PagePlus, you can create your TOC based on your publication's paragraph styles, typically Heading 1, Heading 2, and Heading 3. Although one TOC may normally suffice, there's no limit on the number of TOCs you can create.

Different type of publication may use TOCs in different ways:

- **Technical**. A Table of Figures could be created that lists technical drawings.

- **Financial**. A Table of Figures could be created that lists tables and flow charts.

- **Illustrated**. A Table of Illustrations could be created that lists pictures or graphics.

- **Procedural**. A TOC could be created that lists procedure headings.

- **Multi-chapter**. As well as a main TOC at the start of your publication, a partial TOC could be added at each chapter start.

Irrespective of use, all TOCs can be created by using the TOC tab. It helps you create one or more TOCs derived from any named paragraph styles in your publication (if checked in the tab).

You'll need to assign text styles to your publication's text before you can generate your TOC. See Working with named styles on p. 134.

If you're publishing to PDF, PagePlus can automatically build a bookmark list using the same style markings in your text.

To display the TOC tab:

- From the **Insert** menu, choose **Table of Contents....**
  - or -

- From the **View** menu, select **Studio Tabs**, then click **TOC tab**.

To create a new table of contents:

1. From the TOC tab, check which named paragraph styles you want to base your TOC on.

☐ Heading	☐
☑ Heading 1	☑
☑ Heading 2	☑
☑ Heading 3	☑
☐ Heading 4	☐

   The check boxes at the right can be unchecked to prevent associated page numbers from being shown.

2. (Optional) Create an insertion in your publication text if you want to place your TOC at a certain position. Otherwise, the TOC is placed at the start of your story text.

3. From the tab's drop-down list, select <New...>.

4. From the dialog, enter a TOC **Name** (to appear in the drop-down list above), a **Title** (as the TOC's displayed title), a **Style Prefix** (this precedes automatically generated TOC text styles), and then click **OK**.

In reality, you'll probably generate your TOC and immediately spot a mistake in your TOC's referenced text! To resolve, you can edit the text in your publication and regenerate your TOC.

To regenerate your TOC:

- From the control bar of the selected TOC, click   **Regenerate**. The TOC text is replaced with newer referenced text.

> Whenever you publish to PDF or ePub, you'll be prompted to regenerate any TOCs present.

For electronic PDF delivery, you can optionally hyperlink each page number to its actual page location.

To add hyperlinks to your TOC:

- Click   **Add hyperlinks**.

To delete a TOC:

- From the control bar of the selected TOC, click   **Delete**.

Tab leaders are a useful visual aid to ""connect" the TOC text with its page reference. This help you look up the correct page for specific content.

To add (or modify) a tab leader:

- Click   **Tab Leader** and select a leader style.

Creating multiple Tables of Contents

Instead of a single TOC at the start of your publication that shows all TOC references throughout, PagePlus can create and insert multiple TOCs at specific points throughout your publication. Each subsequent TOC will each reference up to the end of the publication from that TOC position, and is created in the same way as described above.

A powerful way of using multiple TOCs is to make your 2nd, 3rd, 4th TOCs **partial**. With **Partial Table of Contents** enabled on a specific TOC, only items up to the next placed TOC will be shown in that TOC. This is useful when adding "mini" TOCs at every chapter start, which just display that chapter's references. For example, TOCs named Chpt1_TOC, Chpt2_TOC, and Chpt3_TOC could be set to partial.

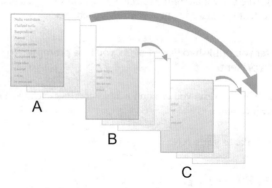

(A) MainTOC, (B) Chpt1_TOC, (C) Chpt2_TOC.

To switch off this setting for a selected TOC, click **Partial Table of Contents**. The TOC will automatically regenerate to include references up to the end of your publication.

Changing table of contents style

When any table of contents is created, PagePlus formats it using built-in text styles (p. 132) intended specifically for table of contents preparation: "Contents-Title" and "Contents-1st" through "Contents-6th". You can easily change the look of your table of contents by changing the style definitions for these built-in "Contents" styles.

Additional TOCs can be assigned different style names on creation, using a Style Prefix setting, e.g. "Chpt1_Contents".

Creating an index

An **index** is a valuable reader aid in a longer document such as a report or manual. PagePlus lets you create an index with **main entries** and **subentries**, based on **index marks** you insert in frame, table, or artistic text. Your index is typically placed at the end of your publication and is made up of index entries and associated page references.

Index marks can be created and inserted into your publication text from the **Index tab**. The tab also lets you navigate your index marks as well as generate your index once you've finished adding index marks.

To display the Index tab:

- From the Insert menu, choose **Index...**.
  - or -

- From the View menu, select **Studio Tabs**, then click **Index Tab**.

To mark individual index entries:

1. Select a portion of text or click for an insertion point before (or within) the first word you want to mark.

2. From the Index tab, click ⬛ **Mark Index Entry**.

3. From the dialog, add your index entry in the **Main entry** or **Subentry** box. If you selected a word or phrase in the story, it appears as the Main entry in the dialog. You can use the entry as it is, or type new text for the main entry and Sub-entry (if any). You must include a main entry for each sub-entry.

4. For a standard index entry, leave the **Current page** box enabled. Enable **Cross-reference** to cross-reference from one index entry to another.

5. Click **Mark** to insert the new entry mark or update a selected mark. The index entry is added to the page (you'll need to display index marks to see the indexed text).

To display index marks:

- From the **Hintline** toolbar, select ¶ ▾ **Show Special Characters**, and select **Index Marks**.

All index marks will be displayed throughout your publication in curly brackets (and in a blue colour), e.g. {battery}.

If you're using the same term repeatedly throughout your publication, PagePlus lets you mark every instance of the word (phrase) to be indexed all at the same time.

To mark all index entries:

1. Select a portion of text or click for an insertion point before (or within) the word you want to mark.

2. From the Index tab, click 🔳 **Mark All Index Entries**.

3. From the dialog, you'll see a list of entries using the same term.

4. Click **Mark** to index them simultaneously.

To jump to an index mark:

1. Expand the index entry by clicking ▶, then select the page reference.

2. Click 📄 **Go To Entry**. The index mark is selected, and is ready to be edited.

To delete an index entry:

- Select an index entry, and click 🔳 **Delete Entry**.

Generating an index

Once you've completed adding all your index marks, they all need to be collated into a single self-contained index, typically placed at the back of your publication.

To generate an index:

1. From the Index tab, click 📇 **Generate Index**.

2. From the **Generate Index** dialog, add a **Title** that will show as your index title.

3. In the Placement section, select whether to place your index in a text frame on a new page at either the end or beginning of your publication.

4. Choose how to format your index.

   To generate an index for an entire book (as set up with BookPlus), select **Index entire book**.

5. Repeat at any time to update the information.

Changing index style

In a similar way to tables of contents, when any index is created, PagePlus includes four built-in text styles intended specifically for use in an index: "Index-Main", "Index-Separator", "Index-Sub", and "Index-Title". You can update the Index styles as needed (see Using text styles on p. 132).

Producing a book with BookPlus

BookPlus is a management utility built into PagePlus that lets you produce a whole book from a set of separate PagePlus (*.ppp) publication files. Using BookPlus, you can arrange the chapter files in a specific order, systematically renumber pages, synchronize styles and other elements between all chapters, create a Table of Contents and/or Index for the whole book, and output the book via printing, PostScript®, or PDF. BookPlus can perform all these managerial tasks whether or not the original files are open! Your settings are saved as a compact BookPlus (*.ppb) book file, separate from the source publication files.

Working with books and chapters

A book consists of a set of PagePlus (*.ppp) publication files. Each publication file is considered a chapter in the book. To create a new book, you'll need at least one constituent chapter file.

To create a new book:

- In PagePlus, on the **File** menu, choose **New** and then click **New Book...**.

BookPlus opens with an empty dialog reserved for the **chapter list**.

To add a chapter to the chapter list:

1. In BookPlus, on the **Standard** toolbar, click [icon] **Add....**

2. In the dialog, select one or more PagePlus files to be added as chapters. (Use the **Ctrl** or **Shift** keys to select multiple files or a range of files.) Click **Open.**

The selected files appear in the chapter list, which can be reordered by dragging.

> Once you've created a chapter list, you can add new chapters at any time, or replace/remove chapters in the current list from the **Standard** toolbar.

To save the current chapter list as a book file:

*   Choose [icon] Save (or **Save As...**) from the BookPlus **Standard** toolbar.

> You can open saved book files from PagePlus using **File>Open....** You can have more than one book file open at a time.

Numbering pages

BookPlus provides a variety of options for incrementing page numbers continuously from one chapter to another, through the whole book. Page numbers will only appear on pages or (more commonly) master pages where you've inserted page number fields. To "suppress" page numbers—for example, on a title page—simply don't include a page number field there.

BookPlus lets you change page number style choices you've made in the original file (using **Format/Page Number Format...** in PagePlus), and provides other options such as inserting a blank page when necessary to force new chapters to start on a right-hand page. You don't need to have the original files open to update page numbering.

To set page numbering options for the book:

1. Choose **Book Page Number Options...** from the BookPlus File menu.

2. In the dialog, select whether you want page numbers to **Continue from previous chapter**, **Continue on next odd page**, or **Continue on next even page**. Typically you'll want new chapters to start on odd (right-hand or "recto") pages.

3. Leave **Insert blank page when necessary** checked if you want to output an extra page at the end of a chapter where the next page number (if you've selected odd- or even-page continuation) would otherwise skip a page. Either way, BookPlus will number your pages correctly—but for correct imposition in professional printing it's usually best to insert the blank page. **Note:** You won't see the blank page inserted into your original file, only in the generated output.

4. Click **OK**. BookPlus immediately applies your settings to all chapters.

To set page numbering options for a chapter:

- Select its name in the list and choose **Chapter Page Number Options...** from the Chapter menu.

The **Page Number Format** dialog displays current settings for numbering style and initial numbering for the chapter (or for any sections created within that chapter if you want to use mixed page number formats per section). (See Using page numbering on p. 44 for more details.)

If you've reordered chapters or changed the chapter list in any way, you can quickly reimpose correct numbering on the current list.

To update page numbering:

- Choose **Renumber Pages** from the BookPlus File menu.

Synchronizing chapters

Synchronizing means imposing consistent styles, palettes, and/or colour schemes throughout the book. This is accomplished by using one chapter (called the **style source**) as a model for the rest of the book. You define attributes in the style source chapter, and then select which attributes should be adjusted in other chapters to conform to the style source. For example, you could redefine the "Normal" text style in your style source chapter, then quickly propagate that change through the rest of the book. The Modified and Synchronized columns of the BookPlus chapter list let you keep track of recent file changes.

To set one chapter as the style source:

- Select its name in the chapter list and choose **Set Style Source** from the Chapter menu.

The current style source is identified in the Synchronized column of the chapter list.

To synchronize one or more chapters with the style source:

1. To update just certain chapters, make sure their names are selected in the chapter list.

2. Choose **Synchronize...** from the **File** menu.

3. In the dialog, select whether you want to update **All** or just **Selected** chapters. Check which attributes should be updated to conform to those defined in the style source file: **Text styles**, **Object styles**, **Colour scheme**, and/or **Colour palette**.

4. Click **OK**.

BookPlus imposes the specified changes and updates the Synchronized time in the chapter list for each selected file. If the file was altered in any way, the Modified time updates as well.

Building a Table of Contents or Index

From BookPlus, you can build a **Table of Contents** and/or **Index** that includes entries for the entire set of chapters. For an index, index entries must first be marked in each individual document (see Creating an index on p. 169). You'll need to begin by designating a specific chapter where the resulting pages should be added.

To create a table of contents for the book:

1. In the chapter list, select the name of the chapter file where you want to add the table of contents.

2. Choose **Insert** from the Chapter menu and select **Table of Contents....**

    BookPlus opens the chapter file if it's not already open, and the **Table of Contents** Wizard appears.

3. Select **Yes** when the Wizard asks if you want to build a table of contents for the entire book. Continue clicking **Next>** and selecting choices in the Wizard.

To create an index for the book:

1. In the chapter list, select the name of the chapter file where you want to add the index.

2. Choose **Insert** from the Chapter menu and select **Index**.

3. BookPlus opens the chapter file if it's not already open, and displays the **Index** tab to help you build and generate the index. Ensure you select **Index entire book** in the **Generate Index** dialog. (See Creating an index on p. 169.)

Printing and PDF output

When you **print** or generate **PDF output** from BookPlus, you'll have the choice of printing the entire book or selected chapters, including all, odd, or even pages.

To print or create a PDF from the book or selected chapters:

1. (Optional) To print just certain chapters, make sure their names are selected in the chapter list.

2. Choose 🖶 **Print Book** or 🛆 **Publish as PDF** from the BookPlus **Standard** toolbar.

3. From the dialog, under **Range**, select **Entire Book** to output all chapters, **Selected Chapters** to output just those you selected previously, or enter specific page numbers or ranges. Whichever option you've chosen, the **Include** drop-down list lets you print all sheets in the range, or just odd or even sheets.

For printing, set other options as detailed in Printing basics on p. 258, then click **Print**. For PDF output, set options as detailed in Exporting PDF files on p. 261, then click **OK**.

Hyperlinking an object

Hyperlinking an object such as a box, a word, or a picture means that a reader of your published PDF document (or visitor to your published HTML pages) can trigger an event by clicking on the object. The event might be a jump to a different page, the appearance of an email composition window, the display of a graphic, text, or media file, or a jump to an anchor (p. 97) attached to a target object.

To hyperlink an object:

1. Use the **Pointer Tool** to highlight the region of text, or select an object (individual or grouped).

2. Click 🔗 **Hyperlink** on the **Standard** toolbar.

3. In the **Hyperlinks** dialog, click to select the link destination type, and enter the specific hyperlink target—an Internet page, a page in your publication/website, an email address, local file, or an object's anchor on p. 97.

4. Click **OK**.

As a visual cue, hyperlinked words are underlined and appear in the colour you've specified (as the Hyperlink colour) in your publication's current colour scheme.

To modify or remove a hyperlink:

1. Right-click the object and select **Edit Hyperlink** (or **Hyperlink**).

2. From the **Hyperlinks** dialog, which opens with the current link target shown, either:

   - To modify the hyperlink, select a new link destination type and/or target.

   - To remove the hyperlink, click the **Remove** button.

For a "birds-eye" view of all the hyperlinks in your publication, use the **Hyperlink Manager** (**Tools** menu).

Viewing hyperlinks in your publication

The **Hyperlink Manager** gives you an overview of all the hyperlinks in your publication.

Page	Hyperlink	Linked to
Page 1	Text "Aenean"	Anchor: Page 2#ExamplePicture
Page 1	Text "Lorem ipsum "	URL: http://www.rome.it
Page 1	DSCN0192.JPG - Emb. Bitmap	URL: http://www.image.com

To display the Hyperlink Manager:

- Choose **Hyperlink Manager...** from the **Tools** menu.

The Hyperlink Manager dialog displays both object and text hyperlinks in your publication, listed by page number. The entries show each link's source object type (Text, Embedded bitmap, etc.) and its destination page, anchor name, or URL

To display a hyperlink for closer inspection:

- Click to select the link entry and click the **Display** button.

To remove or modify a hyperlink:

- Click to select the link entry and click the **Remove** or **Modify** button. To modify the hyperlink, select a new link destination type and/or target.

Using mail merge

Most commonly, **mail merge** means printing your publication a number of times, inserting different information each time from a **data source** such as an address list file—for example into a series of letters or mailing labels.

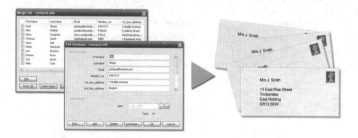

PagePlus can handle many kinds of data sources and more challenging creative tasks. It is even possible to merge picture data (for example, digital photos) into single fields or even auto-create a grid layout of pictures and text suitable for catalogs or photo albums.

As mail merge is an advanced feature of PagePlus, see PagePlus Help for more details. Subjects covered include:

- Opening a data source.

- Editing Serif Database files.

- Selecting, filtering, and sorting the merge list.

- Inserting placeholders for your data.

- Previewing data in the publication.

- Merging and printing.

8 **Working with Pictures, Lines, and Shapes**

Adding picture frames

Picture frames let you present your pictures in a decorative surround, much like you'd show off your favourite picture in a picture frame in your home. You can select from an impressive collection of professionally designed picture frames, and simply drag them onto your publication page before filling them with pictures.

Picture frames are assets, along with graphics, pictures, page elements, backgrounds, and are browsed for (and managed) in the same way as any other asset. See Using assets on p. 67.

To add a picture frame:

1. From the Assets tab, select **Browse**....

2. In the **Asset Browser** dialog, select **Picture Frames** from the **Categories** section.

3. Navigate the themed sub-categories to locate a picture frame, then select an individual frame or click **Add All** to include all the frames from the sub-category. A check mark will appear on selected thumbnails.

4. Click **Close**. The frame(s) appears in the **Assets** tab (Picture Frames category).

5.   Drag a chosen frame thumbnail to your page.

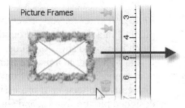

> Empty picture frames are shown as envelope-shaped placeholders on
> the page.

To add a borderless picture frame:

1.   Select **Rectangular Picture Frame** on the **Tools**
      toolbar's **Picture** flyout.
      - or -
      Select **Picture>Empty Frame...** from the **Insert** menu.

2.   The mouse pointer changes to the **Picture Paste** cursor. What
      you do next determines the initial size and placement of the picture
      frame.

      - To insert the frame at a default size, simply click the mouse.
        - or -

      - To set the size of the frame, drag out a region and release the
        mouse button. If needed, use the **Shift** key while dragging to
        maintain aspect ratio (to a square).

> Picture frames can also be applied to objects such as text frames and
> tables. These are considered to be borders, and can be manipulated
> further with respect to width, edge selection, and edge alignment. See
> Adding borders in PagePlus Help.

To add a picture to a frame (and vice versa):

- From the Assets tab (Pictures category), drag and drop a picture directly onto the picture frame.

- or -

- From the Assets tab (Picture Frames category), drag and drop a picture frame directly onto an already placed picture.

The picture is added to the frame using default Picture Frame properties, i.e. it is scaled to maximum fit; aspect ratio is always maintained. However, you can alter the picture's size, orientation, positioning, and scaling relative to its frame.

To change picture size and positioning:

 All selected picture frames that contain a picture will display a supporting **Picture frame** toolbar under the frame. This offers panning, rotation (90 degrees anti-clockwise), zoom in, zoom out, and replace picture controls).

To change picture scaling and alignment:

1. Select the picture frame and choose ▦ **Frame Properties** on the Picture context toolbar.

2. In the dialog, you can scale to maximum/minimum, Stretch to Fit, or use the original image's size (No Scale).

3. To change vertical alignment of pictures within the frames, select **Top**, **Middle**, or **Bottom**.

4. For horizontal alignment, select **Left**, **Centre**, or **Right**.

Creating shaped picture frames

While you can take advantage of PagePlus's preset frames you can create your own shape (e.g., a morphed QuickShape or closed curve) then convert it to a picture frame.

To create a shaped picture frame:

1. Create a closed shape or QuickShapes (p. 206 and p. 204, respectively).

2. Right-click the shape and select **Convert To>Picture Frame**.

You can then add a picture to the frame as described previously.

> Any object you've designed that contains a "hole" can be converted to a picture frame using the above method.

> To store the picture frame for reuse globally or just in the publication, drag to the Assets tab's My Designs or Picture Frames category. For the latter, if you close the publication, you'll be asked if you want to save the frame to an asset pack. See Storing designs on p. 73.

Adding pictures

The Assets tab (Pictures category) acts as a "basket" for initially gathering together and then including pictures in your publication. Its chief use is to aid the design process by improving efficiency (avoiding having to import pictures one by one) and convenience (making pictures always-at-hand). For picture-rich documents in particular, the tab is a valuable tool for dragging pictures directly into bordered or unbordered picture frames or for simply replacing existing pictures on the page.

PagePlus also lets you insert pictures from a wide variety of file formats, such as bitmaps, vector images, and metafiles (including Serif Metafiles).

For photos from your digital camera, you can simply navigate to the folder containing your already downloaded photos (i.e., on your hard disk) and include them in the tab. Similarly, scanned images already saved to your hard disk can be added by this method.

Adding pictures to the Assets tab

To add pictures to the tab:

1.   Select the Assets tab's Pictures category, and click **Add...**

2.   From the dialog, navigate to a folder, and select your picture(s).

3.   Click **Open**. Your pictures appear as thumbnails within the Assets tab's Picture category.

To reorder pictures in the tab:

- Select and drag a picture to a new position in the tab.

To delete a picture from the tab:

- Right-click a picture and select **Delete Asset**.

To delete selected pictures:

1.   **Ctrl**-click or **Shift**-click to select non-adjacent or adjacent pictures.

2.   Right-click any selected picture, and select **Delete Assets**.

To delete all pictures:

1.   Right-click a picture and select **Select All**.

2.   Right-click again, and select **Delete Assets**.

Adding pictures to the page

Pictures can be added to your publication by dragging directly onto your page.

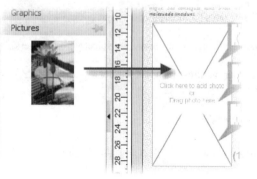

To add a picture to your page:

- From the Assets tab (Pictures category), drag a picture thumbnail directly onto the page, inline into artistic/frame text (at a chosen insertion point), or into a picture frame.

  ① Once added, the picture thumbnail indicates the number of times the picture has been used in the publication.

> When placed, pictures are linked to your project by default and not embedded. Photos can be embedded instead on import via the **Tools** toolbar or at any time using the Resource Manager.

If you've positioned empty picture frames you can use **AutoFlow** to automatically populate them with pictures.

AutoFlow—adding content automatically

AutoFlow lets you flow the pictures present in the tab's Pictures category throughout empty picture **frames** spread throughout your publication (you can't reflow pictures once frames are populated with content).

To automatically flow your pictures:

- Click **AutoFlow** at the bottom of the Assets tab (Pictures category). The pictures are placed sequentially in your document's available picture frames in the order they appear in the tab (reorder beforehand if needed).

Searching for tagged pictures

PagePlus lets you retrieve pictures by individual **tag**, i.e. XMP metadata stored within each picture. You can tag photos by using the Asset Manager.

To search for pictures by tag:

- Click in the search box at the bottom of the Assets tab and enter a search term, e.g. holiday. Matching pictures will appear directly above the search box in a temporary Search Results tab.

Adding pictures with resizing and embed/link control

As well as dragging a picture thumbnail from the Assets tab, pictures can be added to PagePlus by copy and paste or dragging a file from an external Windows folder directly onto your page.

PagePlus also lets you import pictures via ![icon] **Import Picture...** on the **Tools** toolbar. You'll be able to size the picture and embed/link the picture in your publication. See PagePlus Help for more information.

Using Cutout Studio

Cutout Studio offers a powerful integrated solution for cutting objects out from their backgrounds. Depending on the make up of your images you can separate subject of interests from their backgrounds, either by retaining the subject of interest (usually people, objects, etc.) or removing a simple uniform background (e.g., sky, studio backdrop). In both instances, the resulting "cutout" image creates an eye-catching look for your publication.

The latter background removal method is illustrated in the following multi-image example.

The white initial background is discarded, leaving interim checkerboard transparency, from which another image can be used as a more attractive background. A red tint on the second image's background is used to indicate areas to be discarded.

To launch Cutout Studio:

1. Select a picture to be cut out.

2. Select ![icon] Cutout Studio from the displayed Picture context toolbar. Cutout Studio is launched.

Choose an output

It's essential that you choose an output type prior to selecting areas for keeping/discarding. Either an alpha-edged or vector-cropped bitmap can be chosen as your output type prior to selection. The choice you make really depends on the image, in particular how well defined image edges are.

Zoom into your image to examine its edges; this may influence the output type chosen.

Let's look at the output types and explain the difference between each.

Output Type	Description and use
Alpha-edged Bitmap	Use when cutting out objects with poorly defined edges. Transparency and pixel blending are used at the outline edge to produce professional results with negligible interference from background colours. The term "alpha" refers to a 32-bit image's alpha transparency channel.
Vector-cropped Bitmap	Use on more well-defined edges. A cropped image with crop outline is created which can be later manipulated with the crop tools. You can optionally apply feathering to the image edge but will not remove background colour.

You can also set the level of transparency and pixel blending at the cutout edge by adjusting the output settings, Width and Blur. Control of the cutout edge lets you blend your cutout into new backgrounds more realistically.

To create an alpha-edged bitmap:

1. Select **Alpha-edged Bitmap** from the **Output Type** drop-down list.

2. (Optional) Drag the **Width** slider to set the extent to which the "alpha" blending is applied inside the cutout edge. This creates an offset region within which blending occurs.

3. (Optional) Adjust the **Blur** slider to apply a level of smoothing to the region created by the above Width setting.

To create a vector-cropped bitmap:

1. Select **Vector-cropped Bitmap** from the **Output Type** drop-down list.

2. (Optional) Drag the **Feather** slider to apply a soft or blurry edge inside the cutout edge.

3. (Optional) Drag the **Smoothness** slider to smooth out the cutout edge.

4. (Optional) The **Inflate** slider acts as an positive or negative offset from the cutout edge.

You'll need to click ⊙ **Preview** in order to check output setting adjustments each time.

Selecting areas to keep or discard

A pair of brushes for keeping and discarding is used to "paint" areas of the image. The tools are called **Keep Brush** and **Discard Brush**, and are either used independently or, more typically, in combination with each other. When using either tool, the brush paints an area contained by an outline which is considered to be retained or discarded (depending on brush type). A configurable number of pixels adjacent to the outline area are blended.

To aid the selection operation, several display modes are available to show selection.

Show Original, **Show Tinted**, and **Show Transparent** buttons respectively display the image with:

- selection areas only.

- various coloured tints aiding complex selection operations.

- checkerboard transparency areas marked for discarding.

For Show tinted, a red tint indicates areas to be discarded; a green tint shows areas to be kept.

Background colour

For Show transparent mode, a different **Background colour** can be set (at bottom of the Studio) which might help differentiate areas to keep or discard.

To select image areas for keeping/discarding:

1.  In Cutout Studio, click either **Keep Brush Tool** or **Discard Brush Tool** from the left of the Studio workspace.

2. (Optional) Pick a **Brush size** suitable for the area to be worked on.

3. (Optional) Set a **Grow Tolerance** value to automatically expand the selected area under the cursor (by detecting colours similar to those within the current selection). The greater the value the more the selected area will grow. Uncheck the option to switch the feature off.

4. Using the circular cursor, click and drag across the area to be retained or discarded (depending on Keep or Discard Brush Tool selection). It's OK to repeatedly click and drag until your selection area is made.

   The **Undo** button reverts to the last made selection.

To fine-tune your selection, you can switch between Keep and Discard brushes by temporarily holding down the **Alt** key.

5. If you're outputting an alpha-edged bitmap, you can refine the area to be kept/discarded within Cutout Studio (only after previewing) with Erase and Restore touch-up tools. Vector-cropped images can be cropped using standard PagePlus crop tools outside of the Studio.

Make your outline edge as exact as possible by using brush and touch-up tools before committing your work.

6. Click **OK** to create your cutout.

You'll see your image in your publication in its original location, but with the selected areas cut away (made transparent).

Click **Reset** if you want to revert your selected areas and start your cutout again.

Refining your cutout area (alpha-edged bitmaps only)

If a vector-cropped image is created via Image Cutout Studio it's possible to subsequently manipulate the crop outline using crop tools. However, for alpha-edged bitmaps, Erase and Restore touch-up tools can be used to refine the cutout area within the Studio before completing your cutout. The latter can't be edited with crop tools.

Applying PhotoLab filters

Filters can be applied and managed in **PhotoLab**, a powerful studio for applying adjustment and effect filters to pictures individually or in combination—all instantly applied and previewed! PhotoLab offers the following key features:

- **Adjustment filters**
  Apply tonal, colour, lens, and sharpening filters.

- **Effect filters**
  Apply distortion, blur, stylistic, noise, render, artistic and various other effects.

- **Retouching filters**
  Apply red eye correction, spot repair, straightening, and cropping.

- **Non-destructive operation**
  All filters are applied without affecting the original picture, and can be edited at any point in the future.

- **Powerful filter combinations**
  Create combinations of mixed adjustment, retouching, and effect filters for savable work flows.

- **Selective masking**
  Apply filters to selected regions using masks.

- **Save and manage favourites**
  Save filter combinations to a handy **Favourites** tab.

- **Viewing controls**
  Compare before-and-after previews, with dual- and split-screen controls. Use pan and zoom control for moving around your picture.

- **Locking controls**
  Protect your applied filters from accidental change, then optionally apply them to other images on selection.

PhotoLab hosts filter tabs, a main toolbar, and applied filter stack around a central workspace.

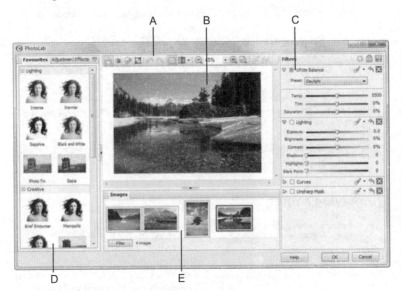

(A) main toolbar, (B) main workspace, (C) filter stack, (D) filter tabs, (E) Images tab

To launch PhotoLab:

1. Select the picture that you want to apply a filter to.

2. Click PhotoLab on the Picture context toolbar.

Using the Images tab

Pictures used in your publication will show in your **Images** tab (above) if the tab is expanded. This tab is shown by default in PhotoLab but can be hidden by clicking the ▬▬▼▬▬ button at the bottom of your workspace.

To search publication images:

1. Click the **Filter** button on the **Images** tab.

2. Select and define a minimum and maximum size, if required.

3. Select or deselect RGB, CMYK and Grayscale to show only images in these colour modes.

4. Click **OK**.

The **Images** tab displays only images which comply to the criteria set above.

> With the Images tab open, you'll be able to select and edit all images without having to exit PhotoLab.

Applying a filter

Filters are stored in PhotoLab's Favourites, Adjustments, and Effects tabs which group filters logically into categories (e.g., Quick Fix for fast and commonly used correction filters).

The Favourites tab offers some commonly used filters (individual and in combination). You can complement these with your own user-defined filters.

To apply a filter with trialling:

1. Click a filter thumbnail.

2. As soon as a filter is selected it is temporarily added to **Trial Zone** which lets you experiment freely with your own settings for that filter; the picture automatically refreshes to preview your new settings.

3. Adjust sliders (or enter input values) until your filter suits your requirements. Some filters offer check boxes, drop-down lists, and additional controls (e.g., Advanced settings).

> Selecting a new filter always replaces the current filter.

Any filter can be temporarily disabled, reset, or deleted from the trial zone.

To disable: Click ▣. Click ☐ to enable again.

To reset: Click ↰ . Any changes to settings are reverted back to the filter's defaults.

To delete: Click ☒ .

Once you're sure that you want to keep your filter, you'll need to commit the filter to your filters stack.

To commit your filter:

• Click ⊜ **Commit** to accept your changes. This adds the filter to the right-most **Filters** stack where additional filters can be added and built up by using the same method.

> Adjustments are applied such that the most recently added filter always appears at the bottom of the list and is applied to the picture last (after the other filters above it).

To reorder filters:

- Drag and drop your filter into any position in the stack. A dotted line indicates the new position in which the entry will be placed on mouse release.

To add a filter directly (without trialling):

- Click ⬡ **Add Quick Filter** at the top of the Filters stack and choose a filter from the flyout categories. The filter is applied directly to the stack without trialling.

Retouching

PhotoLab offers some useful retouching tools on the main toolbar, each commonly used to correct photos before applying colour correction and effects.

Selective masking

Rather than apply a filter to uniformly change the appearance of your picture, you can change only selected regions instead. PhotoLab lets you mask picture areas by painting areas to be either affected by filters or simply left alone.

To apply a mask:

1. From the 🖌 ▾ **Mask** drop-down list, select **New Mask**.

2. In the Tool Settings pane, select the 🖌 **Add Region** tool to allow you to mask regions by painting.

3. Adjust the settings to suit requirements, especially adjusting Brush Size to paint larger or more intricate regions.

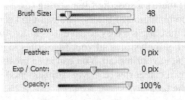

Change the **Mode** drop-down list from Select to Protect to protect painted regions from masking (i.e., the inverse of the Add Region option).

4. Using the on-screen cursor, paint regions (in green for adding; red for protecting).

    If you've not been as accurate as you'd like while painting, you can click **Remove Regions** then paint over the unwanted painted regions.

5. Click ✅ to save your masking changes.

The mask button changes to yellow when a mask is applied.

It's also possible to create additional masks for the same filter as above, and then choose between masks accordingly. You can only have one mask applied at any one time. By using the menu's **New From>** option you can also base the new mask on another mask applied to the current or any other filter in the filter stack. This is useful when using favourites containing multiple adjustments.

To edit a mask:

*   Click the down arrow on the ✏ ▾ button, choose the mask name and select **Edit Mask**.

Saving favourites

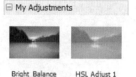

Bright_Balance   HSL Adjust 1

HSL Adjust 2

If there's a specific filter setting (or combination of filters) you want to keep for future use it's easy to save it as a **favourite**. PhotoLab stores all your favourites together in the Favourites tab. You can even create your own categories (e.g. My Adjustments) within the tab.

To save filter(s) as a new favourite:

- Click 💾 **Save Filter**.

- From the dialog, enter a favourite name and pick a category to save the filter to.

  Click 🔲 to create new category.

▽ If you want to further manage your favourites into user-defined categories, click the option on the **Tab Menu**.

Drawing and editing lines

PagePlus provides **Pencil**, **Straight Line**, and **Pen** tools for drawing freehand, straight, and curved/straight lines, respectively.

The ✏ **Pencil Tool** lets you sketch curved lines and shapes in a **freeform** way. See PagePlus Help for more details.

The ✒ **Pen Tool** lets you join a series of line segments (which may be **curved** or **straight**) using "connect the dots" mouse clicks. See PagePlus Help for more details.

The ✎ **Straight Line Tool** is for drawing **straight** lines (for example, drawn in the column gutter to separate columns); rules at the top and/or bottom of the page; or horizontal lines to separate sections or highlight headlines.

> ★ Any curved line can be closed (by joining line ends) to create a custom **shape** (see Drawing and editing shapes on p. 204 for details).

To draw a straight line (with the Straight Line Tool):

1. Choose the ✎ **Straight Line Tool** from the **Tools** toolbar.

2. Click where you want the line to start, and drag to the end point. The line appears immediately.

> ★ To constrain the angle of the straight line to 15° increments, hold down the **Shift** key as you drag. (This is an easy way to make exactly vertical or horizontal lines.)

3. To extend the line, position the cursor over one of its end nodes. The cursor changes to include a plus symbol. Click on the node and drag to add a new line segment.

Editing lines

Use the Pointer Tool in conjunction with the Curve context toolbar to adjust lines once you've drawn them. The techniques are the same whether you're editing a separate line object or the outline of a closed shape.

When selected, each line type shows square nodes which can be used for reshaping lines.

See PagePlus Help for information on editing lines.

Setting line properties

All lines, including those that enclose shapes, have numerous properties, including colour, weight (width or thickness), scaling, cap (end), join (corner), and stroke alignment. You can vary these properties for any freehand, straight, or curved line, as well as for the outline of a shape. Note that text frames, pictures, tables, and artistic text objects have line properties too.

To change line properties of a selected object:

- Use the ▇ Line swatch on the Swatches tab to change the line's colour and/or shade. Alternatively, use the equivalent swatch on the Colour tab to apply a line colour from a colour mixer.

  The object's line and fill can take a solid or gradient colour, as well as bitmaps and transparency effects.

- Use the Line tab, context toolbar (shown when a line is selected), or Line and Border dialog to change the line's weight (thickness), type, or other properties. Select a line width, and use the drop-down boxes to pick the type of line. The context toolbar can also adjust line-end scaling as a percentage.

On the **Line** tab, context toolbar, or Line and Border dialog, the styles drop-down list provides the following styles: **None**, **Single**, **Calligraphic**, and several **Dashed** and **Double** line styles as illustrated below.

Several techniques offer additional ways to customize lines:

 (Tab and dialog only) Drag the **Dash Pattern** slider to set the overall pattern length (the number of boxes to the left of the slider) and the dash length (the number of those boxes that are black).

The illustrations below show lines with pattern and dash lengths of (1) 4 and 2, and (2) 5 and 4:

 (Tab only) For calligraphic lines of variable width (drawn as if with a square-tipped pen held at a certain angle), select the calligraphic line style (opposite) from the drop-down list, then use the **Calligraphic Angle** box to set the angle of the pen tip, as depicted in the examples below.

You can also vary a line's **Cap** (end) and the **Join** (corner) where two lines intersect.

Drawing and editing shapes

QuickShapes are pre-designed objects of widely varying shapes that you can instantly add to your page.

Once you've drawn a QuickShape, you can morph its original shape using control handles, and adjust its properties—for example, by applying gradient or bitmap fills (including your own bitmap pictures!) or transparency effects.

Another way to create a shape is to draw a line (or series of line segments) and then connect its start and end nodes, creating a closed shape.

QuickShapes

The QuickShape flyout contains a wide variety of commonly used shapes, including boxes, ovals, arrows, polygons, stars, cubes, and cylinders.

You can easily turn shapes into web **buttons** by adding hyperlinks or overlaying hotspots. The "Quick Button" (indicated) is especially intended for creating stylish button outlines!

It's also possible to use the always-at-hand QuickShape context toolbar situated above the workspace to adjust a QuickShape's line weight, colour, style, and more. New shapes always take the default line and fill (initially a black line with a white fill).

To create a QuickShape:

1. Click the 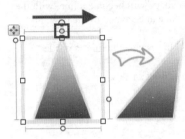 **QuickShape** flyout on the **Tools** toolbar and select a shape from the flyout.

2. Click on the page to create a new shape at a default size.
   - or -
   Drag across the page to size your shape. When the shape is the right size, release the mouse button.

To draw a constrained shape (such as a circle):

- Hold down the **Shift** key as you drag.

All QuickShapes can be positioned, resized, rotated, and filled. What's more, you can morph them using adjustable sliding handles around the QuickShape. Each shape changes in a logical way to allow its exact appearance to be altered.

To adjust the appearance of a QuickShape:

1. Click on the QuickShape to reveal one or more sliding handles around the shape. These are distinct from the "inner" selection handles. Different QuickShapes have different handles which have separate functions.

2. To change the appearance of a QuickShape, drag its handles.

To find out what each handle does for a particular shape, move the Pointer Tool over the handle and read the Hintline.

Closed shapes

As soon as you draw or select a line, you'll see the line's nodes appear. Nodes show the end points of each segment in the line. Freehand curves typically have many nodes; straight or curved line segments have only two. You can make a shape by extending a line back to its starting point.

To turn a selected line into a shape:

- Select the line with the **Pointer Tool** and then click the ⬚ **Close Curve** button on the Curve context toolbar.

You can go the other way, too—break open a shape in order to add one or more line segments.

To break open a line or shape:

1. With the **Pointer Tool**, select the node where you want to break the shape.

2. Click the ⬚ **Break Curve** button on the Curve context toolbar. A line will separate into two lines. A shape will become a line, with the selected node split into two nodes, one at each end of the new line.

3. You can now use the **Pointer Tool** to reshape the line as needed.

See PagePlus Help for more information on editing shapes.

Saving custom shapes

Having taken time to create your custom shapes, you may wish to reuse them in future projects. The **Assets** tab provides the ideal location for storing your custom shapes for later use.

To add custom shapes to the Assets tab:

1. On the **Assets** tab, click the **My Designs** category header.

2. With the **Pointer Tool**, click the bounding box of your shape and drag the shape into the **My Designs** category on the **Assets** tab.

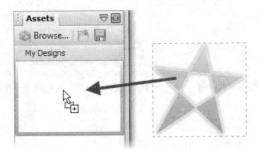

The shape is stored in the **Assets** tab and is accessible for all future projects.

Your custom shape can also be added to the **Asset** tab's **Picture Frames** category. This will automatically convert your shape into picture frame. See Adding picture frames (p. 183) and Storing designs (p. 73) for more information.

Applying 2D filter effects

PagePlus provides a variety of **filter effects** that you can use to transform any object. "3D" filter effects let you create the impression of a textured surface and are covered on p. 211. Here we'll look at 2D filter effects exclusively. The following examples show each 2D filter effect when applied to the letter "A."

Drop Shadow

Inner Shadow

Outer Glow

Inner Glow

Inner Bevel

Outer Bevel

Emboss

Pillow Emboss

Gaussian Blur

Zoom Blur

Radial Blur

Motion Blur

Colour Fill

Feather

Outline

Reflection

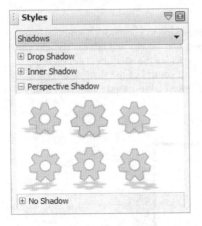

The Studio's Styles tab offers a range of 2D filter effects that are ready to use. Its multiple categories each offer a gallery full of predefined effects, such as Shadows, Bevels, Reflections, Blurs, and more. Each category offers subtle variations of the category effect. Click any thumbnail to apply the effect to the selected object.

PagePlus additionally provides the Shadow Tool for applying a shadow to an object directly in your publication. Control handles let you adjust shadow blur, opacity and colour.

For absolute control over your 2D filter effects, you can use *fx* **Filter Effects**.

To apply 2D filter effects:

1. Select an object and click the *fx* **Filter Effects** button on the **Attributes** toolbar.

2. To apply a particular effect, check its box in the list on the left.

3. To adjust the properties of a specific effect, select its name and vary the dialog controls. Adjust the sliders or enter specific values to vary the combined effect. (You can also select a slider and use the keyboard arrows.) Options differ from one effect to another.

4. Click **OK** to apply the effect or **Cancel** to abandon changes.

Using the Shadow Tool

Shadows are great for adding flair and dimension to your work, particularly to pictures and text objects, but also to shapes, text frames and tables. To help you create them quickly and easily, PagePlus provides the **Shadow Tool** on the **Attributes** toolbar. The tool affords freeform control of the shadow effect allowing creation of adjustable **basic** or **skewed edge-based shadows** for any PagePlus object.

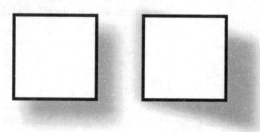

Basic (left) and skewed shadows (right) applied to a basic square QuickShape

Adjustment of shadow colour, opacity, blur, and scaling/distance is possible using controllable nodes directly on the page (or via a supporting Shadow context toolbar). Nodes can be dragged inwards or outwards from the shadow origin to modify the shadow's blur and opacity. For a different colour, pick a new colour from the Colour or Swatches tab while the tool is selected. Depending on if a basic or skewed shadow is required, the origin can exist in the centre (shown) or at the edge of an object, respectively.

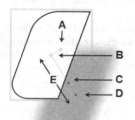

(A) Blur, (B) Shadow origin, (C) Opacity, (D) Colour, (E) Scaling

Once you've created a shadow, you can also fine-tune it as needed using the Filter Effects dialog.

Using 3D filter effects

3D filter effects go beyond 2D filter effects (such as shadow, glow, bevel, and emboss effects) to create the impression of a textured surface on the object itself. You can use the **Filter Effects** dialog to apply one or more effects to the same object. Keep in mind that none of these 3D effects will "do" anything to an unfilled object—you'll need to have a fill there to see the difference they make!

The Studio's Styles tab is a good place to begin experimenting with 3D filter effects. Its multiple categories each offers a gallery full of pre-defined mixed 2D and 3D effects, using various settings.

There you'll see a variety of remarkable 3D surface and texture presets in various categories (Presets - Default, Presets - Fun, Presets - Materials, and Texture). The Presets - Materials category offers realistic effects such as Glass, Metallic, Wood, etc. Click any thumbnail to apply it to the selected object. Assuming the object has some colour on it to start with, you'll see an instant result!

fx Alternatively, you can customize a Styles tab preset, or apply one or more specific effects from scratch, by using **Filter Effects** on the **Attributes** toolbar.

Overview

✓ 3D Effects
    3D Bump Map
      Function
         Advanced
    2D Bump Map
    3D Pattern Map
      Function
         Advanced
    2D Pattern Map
    Reflection Map
    Transparency
✓ 3D Lighting

- **3D Effects** is a master switch, and its settings of **Blur** and **Depth** make a great difference; you can click the "+" button to unlink them for independent adjustment.

- **3D Lighting** provides a "light source" without which any depth information in the effect wouldn't be visible. The lighting settings let you illuminate your 3D landscape and vary its reflective properties.

To apply 3D filter effects:

1. Click *fx* **Filter Effects** on the **Attributes** toolbar.

2. Check the **3D Effects** box at the left. The **3D Lighting** box is checked by default.

3. Adjust the "master control" sliders here to vary the overall properties of any individual 3D effects you select.

   - **Blur** specifies the amount of smoothing applied. Larger blur sizes give the impression of broader, more gradual changes in height.

   - **Depth** specifies how steep the changes in depth appear.

   - The ⊞ button is normally down, which links the two sliders so that sharp changes in Depth are smoothed out by the Blur parameter. To adjust the sliders independently, click the button so it's up.

4. Check a 3D effect in the 3D Effects list which reflects the 3D effect you can achieve.

3D Bump Map

The **3D Bump Map** effect creates the impression of a textured surface by applying a mathematical function you select to add depth information, for a peak-and-valley effect. You can use 3D Bump Map in conjunction with one or more additional 3D filter effects—but not with a 2D Bump Map.

2D Bump Map

The **2D Bump Map** effect creates the impression of a textured surface by applying a greyscale bitmap you select to add depth information, for a peak-and-valley effect. You can use 2D Bump Map in conjunction with one or more additional 3D filter effects—but not with a 3D Bump Map.

3D Pattern Map

The **3D Pattern Map** effect creates the impression of a textured surface by applying a mathematical function you select to introduce colour variations. You can use 3D Pattern Map in conjunction with one or more other 3D filter effects.

2D Pattern Map

The **2D Pattern Map** effect creates the impression of a textured surface by applying a greyscale bitmap you select to introduce colour variations. You can use 2D Pattern Map in conjunction with one or more other 3D filter effects.

Reflection Map

The **Reflection Map** effect is used to simulate mirrored surfaces by selection of a pattern (i.e., a bitmap which possesses a shiny surface) which "wraps around" a selected object. Patterns which simulate various realistic indoor and outdoor environments can be adopted, with optional use of 3D lighting to further reflect off object edges.

Transparency

The uniform transparency of an object (with 3D filter effects applied) can be controlled via the Transparency tab (see first example below). However, for more sophisticated transparency control, especially for simulating reflective lighting effects on glass objects, transparency settings can instead be set within the 3D filter effects dialog (check the **Transparency** option). The effect can be used to create more realistic transparency by independently controlling transparency on reflective (edges) and non-reflective (flat) areas of the object (see front heart shape below).

3D Lighting

The **3D Lighting** effect works in conjunction with other 3D effects to let you vary the surface illumination and reflective properties.

Using object styles

Object styles benefit your design efforts in much the same way as text styles and colour schemes. Once you've come up with a set of attributes that you like—properties like line colour, fill, border, and so on—you can save this cluster of attributes as a named style. PagePlus remembers which objects are using that style, and the style appears in the Styles tab, and can subsequently be applied to new objects.

The Styles tab contains multiple galleries of pre-designed styles that you can apply to any object, or customize to suit your own taste! Galleries exist in effect categories such as Blurs, 3D, Edge, Warps, Shadows, Materials (e.g., metals) and more, with each category having further subcategories.

To apply an object style to one or more objects:

1. Display the **Styles** tab.

2. Expand the drop-down list to select a named style category (e.g., Blurs), then pick a subcategory by scrolling the lower window.

3. Preview available styles as thumbnails (cog shapes are shown by default) in the window.

4. Click a style thumbnail to apply it to the selected object(s).

To remove an object style from a gallery:

- Right-click the thumbnail and choose **Delete**.

To unlink an object from its style definition:

- Right-click the object and choose **Format>Object Style>Unlink**.

Saving Object Styles

To create a new object style based on an existing object's attributes:

- Right-click the object and choose **Format>Object Style>Create**.

To save a publication's object styles globally:

1. Choose **Save Defaults...** from the **Tools** menu.

2. From the dialog, check **Object styles**, then click **Save**.

Using connectors

Connector tools let you create dynamic link lines between any two objects. These connectors remain anchored to the objects, even if either or both of them are moved or resized. So, for example, it's easy to create a flow chart with connectors between boxes, then freely rearrange the layout while preserving the directional relationships!

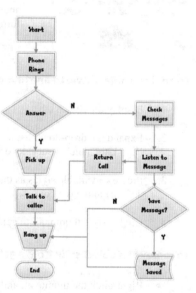

Connector types

The **Elbow Connector Tool** lets you draw a connector with only vertical and horizontal segments—for example, if you're creating a flow chart, organization chart, or tree diagram.

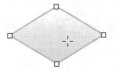 The  **Connector Tool** lets you draw a single, straight-line connector between any two connection points.

Connection points

To make connections easy, each PagePlus object has default square connection points, displayed whenever you select a Connector tool and hover over a target object.

These default points (which can't be moved or deleted) are normally evenly distributed around an object's shape.

To create a connector:

1. Select the **Elbow Connector Tool** from the **Tools** toolbar.

2. (Optional) For a straight-line connector, select the **Connector Tool** on the context toolbar.

3. Hover over an object so that default **connection points** become visible.

4. Drag from the object's connection point to another object's connection point. Release the mouse button when the pointer is over the target connection point. A direct connector will appear between the two connection points.

Instead of using an object's default connection points, you can create your own custom connection points by:

- hovering over any shape's edge and dragging from that red originating point.

Editing connection points and connectors

- To move a custom connection point, select the object to which it is associated and drag the point with the **Connection Point Tool**.

- To delete a custom connection point you've added, use the **Connection Point Tool** to click the object to which the connection point was associated, click the connection point you want to delete, and then press the **Delete** key. Default nodes are fixed and can't be deleted.

- To move, reshape, or detach/reattach a connector, use the **Pointer Tool** to drag individual nodes. Drag the end node of a connector to detach or reattach it. (See Drawing and editing lines on p. 201).

> If you draw a connector with either or both ends unconnected, the free ends stay anchored to the page as drawn. Of course, you can still move, reattach, or edit the connector just as if it were connected to an object.

As connectors are treated as ordinary lines, you can colour them (see p. 221) and format them with the Line tab to add arrows, feathers, or other decorative line end. (See Setting line properties on p. 202.)

9 Colour, Fills, and Transparency

Applying solid fills

PagePlus offers a number of ways to apply solid colour fills to objects of different kinds:

- You can apply solid colours to an object's **line** or **fill**. As you might expect, QuickShapes and closed shapes (see Drawing and editing shapes on p. 204) have both line and fill properties, whereas straight and freehand lines have only a line property.

- Characters in text objects can have fill colour or highlight colour. Text frames and table cells can have a background fill independent of the characters they contain.

- You can colourize a paint-type (bitmap) picture—that is, recolour it to use a different colour. If you recolour a full-colour picture, the colours will convert to tints or shades of the specified colour. You can also apply tinting to a full-colour picture to produce a low-intensity picture (useful for backgrounds behind text).

You can use the Colour tab, Swatches tab or a dialog box to apply solid colours to an object.

To apply a solid colour via the Colour tab:

1. Select the object(s) or highlight a range of text.

2. Click the **Colour** tab and select one of several colour modes (RGB, CMYK, or HSL) from the drop-down list.

3. Click the ▬ **Fill**, ▬ **Line**, or **A** ▬ **Text** button at the top of the tab to determine where colour will be applied. The colour of the underline reflects the colour of your selected object. For selected frame text, the Fill will be the background text colour (but not the frame's background colour).

4. Select a colour from the colour spectrum or sliders depending on colour mode selected.

To apply a solid colour via the Swatches tab:

1. Select the object(s) or highlight a range of text.

2. Click the **Swatches** tab.

3. Click the ⬛ **Fill,** ⬜ **Line,** or **A** **Text** button at the top of the tab to determine where colour will be applied.

4. Select a colour swatch from the **Publication palette** (commonly used colours and those previously applied to your publication) or standard **Palette** (supplied preset swatches).

Alternatively, use **Format>Fill...** to apply colour via a dialog.

To apply a solid colour via the Colours toolbar:

1. Select the object(s) or highlight a range of text.

2. On the **Colours** toolbar, select a colour from the **Fill**, **Line**, or **Text** drop-down lists.

   - or -

   Click the ⬛ **Fill,** ⬛ **Line,** or **A** **Text** button, then in the **Colour Selector** dialog, select a **Colour Model** from the drop-down list and choose a colour from the colour spectrum or sliders depending on colour mode selected. Click **OK**.

> Using the Colours toolbar, you can predefine fill, line, and text colours for future objects. To do this, perform step 2 above without selecting an object first.

To change a solid colour's shade/tint (lightness):

1. Select the object and set the correct Fill, Line or Text button in the Colour tab.

2. From the Colour mode drop-down list, select **Tinting**.

3. Drag the Shade/Tint slider to the left or right to darken or lighten your starting colour, respectively. You can also enter a percentage value in the box (entering 0 in the input box reverts to the original colour).

Adjust the 0% ▶ percentage tinting via slider or direct input to apply object tinting from the Swatches tab.

PagePlus automatically adds used colours to the ▦ **Publication Palette** in the Swatches tab.

You can convert any colour in your palette into a spot colour by selecting the colour's swatch and the **Spot Colour** checkbox in **Palette Manager** (available from the Tools menu).

To change the current palette:

- Click the ▦ ▾ **Palette** button to view and adopt colours from a **Standard RGB**, **Standard CMYK**, or selection of themed palettes. Colours can be added, edited, or deleted from the Publication Palette but not from other palettes.

Using colour schemes

In PagePlus, a **colour scheme** is a cluster of eleven complementary colours (of which **five** are mainly used) that you can apply to specific elements in one or more publications. The **Schemes** tab displays preset schemes (displaying the five main colours) which can be selected at any point during the design process.

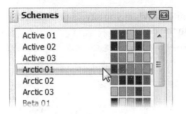

Each publication can have just one colour scheme at a time; the current scheme is highlighted in the **Schemes** tab. You can easily switch schemes, modify scheme colours and create custom schemes. Colour schemes are saved globally, so the full set of schemes is always available.

How colour schemes work

Colour schemes in PagePlus work much like a paint-by-numbers system, where various regions of a layout are coded with numbers, and a specific colour is assigned (by number) to each region. For example, imagine a line drawing coded with the numbers 1 through 5. To fill it in, you'd use paint from jars also numbered 1 through 5. Swapping different colours into the paint jars, while keeping the numbers on the drawing the same, would produce quite a different painting.

In PagePlus, the "paint jars" are numbers you can assign to objects in your publication. They're known as "Scheme Colour 1," "Scheme Colour 2," and so on. When you apply Scheme Colour 1 to an object, it's like saying, "Put the colour from jar number 1 here."

- The **Schemes** tab shows the various available schemes, each with a different set of five colours in the five "jars." Whichever named colour scheme you select, that scheme's first colour (as shown in its sample) will appear in regions defined as Scheme Colour 1, its second colour will map to Scheme Colour 2, and so on throughout the publication.

To select a colour scheme:

1. Click the **Schemes** tab. The currently assigned scheme is highlighted in the list.

2. Click a different colour scheme sample. Objects in the publication that have been assigned one of the colour scheme numbers are updated with the corresponding colour from the new scheme.

You can repeat this selection process indefinitely. When you save a publication, its current colour scheme is saved along with the document.

Applying scheme colours to objects

When you create publications from pre-defined design templates (see p. 20), you can choose the starting colour scheme that you want to adopt; you can always change it later from the **Schemes** tab. This flexibility creates endless possibilities for the look and feel of your publication! However, if you then create new elements in your schemed publication, or start a publication from scratch, how can you extend the current colour scheme to the new objects? Although you'll need to spend some time working out which colour combinations look best, the mechanics of the process are simple. Recalling the paint-by-numbers example above, all you need to do is assign one of the current scheme colour numbers to an object's line and/or fill.

To assign a scheme colour to an object:

1. Select the object and choose a Fill, Line, or **A** Text button at the top of the **Swatches** tab depending on the desired effect.

2. From the bottom of the **Swatches** tab, click on the scheme colour that you want to apply to the fill, line, or text (or you can drag the colour instead).

If an object's fill uses a scheme colour, the corresponding sample in **Swatches** tab will be highlighted whenever the object is selected.

PagePlus lets you create your own scheme by modifying an existing colour scheme or by creating your scheme from scratch. See PagePlus Help for more information.

Creating custom colour schemes

If you've tried various preset colour schemes but haven't found one that's quite right, you can use the **Colour Scheme Designer** to modify any of the colours in an existing scheme (to create a new one) or create your own named scheme from scratch.

Modifying existing colour schemes

To modify a colour scheme:

1. From the Schemes tab, select a colour scheme to be modified from the list.

2. Select **Colour Scheme Designer...** from the **Tools** menu.
    - or -
    Click on the Schemes tab's ▽ **Tab Menu** button and choose **Colour Scheme Designer...** from the drop-down list.

    The **Colour Scheme Designer** dialog appears.

3. From the **Colour Scheme** list at the right of your dialog, each of the scheme colour numbers has its own drop-down list, showing available colours in the PagePlus palette.

    Click the down arrow on the scheme colour you want to modify.

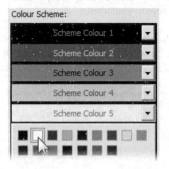

4. Select a new colour from the palette or from the Colour Selector (click **More Colours...**).

5.   Click **OK**. This saves the scheme locally (i.e., just for the publication) and shows in the Swatches tab for easy colour assignment.

To store the modified scheme under a new scheme name in the Schemes tab, jump to the dialog's **Colour Schemes** tab and click **Save As...**. Alternatively, the **Save** option just overwrites the preset. Both options make the new scheme global (available to all new publications).

Creating custom schemes from colour spreads

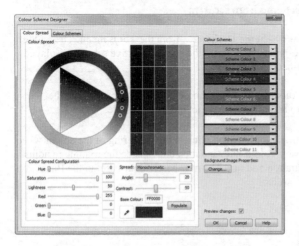

The **Colour Scheme Designer** lets you create eye-catching custom colour schemes from colour spreads.

To start, you choose a **base colour** on which to build your scheme, then you pick from a selection of **colour spreads**—grids of colours based on established colour theory models. Each spread suggests different colour choices for your scheme.

- **Monochromatic** (shown above) - derived from variations of lightness and saturation on the chosen base colour.

- **Complementary** - derived from variations of the base colour and of the colour that sits opposite it on the colour wheel.

- **Triadic** - derived from variations of three colours (one of which is the base colour), spaced equally around the colour wheel.

- **Tetradic** - derived from variations of four colours, arranged around the colour wheel in two complementary colour pairs.

- **Analogous** - derived from variations of colours that are adjacent to each other on the colour wheel, where the centre colour is the base colour.

- **Accented Analogous** - as for **Analogous** but, as for **Complementary**, also includes the colour opposite.

To create a colour scheme from scratch:

1. Select **Colour Scheme Designer...** from the **Tools** menu. The **Colour Scheme Designer** opens, with the currently active scheme displayed in the right-hand scheme list.

2. From the Colour Spread tab, choose a base colour on which the scheme is to be built. Several methods are possible:

   - **Using the colour wheel**: click in the outer ring of the colour wheel to choose a colour hue, and then click inside the triangle to adjust the saturation and tint. The new base colour is set in the Base Colour swatch.

Base Colour: CD2B2B

> The base colour is the colour directly under the marker that sits inside the colour wheel's triangle.

   - **Entering HSL or RGB values**: use the sliders or input boxes to specify a base colour exactly.

- **Drag-and-drop**: drag a colour from the Colour Scheme list onto the colour wheel (or base colour swatch).

- **Using the colour picker**: click and drag the **Colour Picker** to select any on-screen colour.

With any method, the base colour updates to show the new colour.

3. Select a colour spread type from the **Spread** drop-down list.

The colour spread, a grid of suggested colours, updates according to the chosen spread type. The spread offers a range of suggested colours to choose from. The number of colours presented may differ with the spread type.

4. (Optional) Use the **Angle** and/or **Contrast** slider to modify the spread.

5. Once you're happy with the spread colours offered, you can create your scheme either via:

- **one-click**: click the **Populate** button next to the Base colour swatch. The colour scheme is updated automatically with multiple colours.

- **colour-by-colour selection**: drag individual colour(s) from the grid onto a scheme colour on the Colour Scheme list.

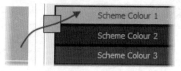

6. To apply the scheme, click **OK**. The colour scheme is now updated and stored in the publication.

> To save the scheme globally so it can be used in other publications, jump to the Colour Schemes tab, then click **Save As....**

Gradient and bitmap fills

Gradient fills provide a gradation or spectrum of colours spreading between two or more points on an object. A gradient fill has an editable path with nodes that mark the origin of each of these key colours. A bitmap fill uses a named bitmap—often a material, pattern, or background image—to fill an object.

Linear   *Elliptical*   *Conical*   *Bitmap*

You can apply preset gradient and bitmap fills from the Swatches tab to the fill or outline of a shape or text frame; table cells as well as artistic, frame, and table text can also take a gradient or bitmap fill. The fill's path on an object's fill or line can also be varied for different effects (see PagePlus Help).

Applying a gradient or bitmap fill

There are several ways to apply a gradient or bitmap fill: using the **Swatches** tab, the **Fill Tool**, or the **Fill** dialog.

The easiest way to apply a gradient or bitmap fill is to use one of a range of pre-supplied swatch thumbnails in the Swatches tab's **Gradient** or **Bitmap** palettes. The **Fill Tool** and a Fill dialog are alternative methods for creating gradient fills.

To apply a gradient or bitmap fill using the Swatches tab:

1. Display the Swatches tab and ensure either **▬** **Fill** or **▢** **Line** is selected (for an object's fill or outline, respectively).
    Note that the colour of the underline reflects the colour of your selected object.

2. ◤ ▾ For gradient fills, select a gradient category, e.g. Linear, Elliptical, etc., from the **Gradient** button's drop-down list.
    - or -
    ▨ ▾ For bitmap fills, select a drop-down list category from the **Bitmap** button.

3. Select the object(s), and then click the appropriate gallery swatch for the fill you want to apply.
    - or -
    For fills only, drag from the gallery swatch onto any object and release the mouse button.

4. If needed, adjust the fill's **Tint** at the bottom of the tab with the tab slider or set a percentage value in the input box.

Applying different transparency effects (using the **Transparency** tab) won't alter the object's fill settings as such, but may significantly alter a fill's actual appearance.

To apply a gradient fill with the Fill Tool:

1. Select an object.

2. Click the  **Fill Tool** on the **Attributes** toolbar.

3. Display the Swatches tab and ensure either ▬ **Fill** or ▭ **Line** is selected (for an object's fill or outline, respectively).

4. Click and drag on the object to define the fill path. The object takes a simple Linear fill, grading from the object's current colour to monochrome white.

> If the object is white already (or has no fill), grading is from white to black.

Alternatively, a dialog can be used to add or subtract **key colours** from the gradient, apply different key colours to individual nodes, or vary the overall shading of the effect applied to the object.

To apply or edit a gradient or bitmap fill using a dialog:

1. Display the Swatches tab and ensure either  **Fill** or  **Line** is selected (for an object's fill or outline, respectively).

2. Right-click the object and choose **Format>Fill**, or select it and choose **Fill...** from the **Format** menu.
   - or -
   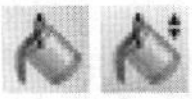 Click the **Fill Tool** on the **Attributes** toolbar and then, on the context toolbar, click **Edit Fill**.

3. Choose the fill type and the desired fill category. Note that you can also use the dialog to apply a solid fill.

   - For gradient fills, select **Gradient** from the **Type** drop-down list, and pick a gradient preset. A two-colour gradient has two nodes, one at each end of its path.
     - or -
     Click the **From** and **To** buttons to specify the gradient's start and end colours.
     - or -
     Click the **Edit** button if you want to add or subtract key colours from the currently chosen gradient, apply different key colours to individual nodes, or vary the overall shading of the effect applied to the object. You can adjust the fill's shade/tint as needed using the drop-down list.

   - For bitmap fills, select **Bitmap** from the **Type** drop-down list, choose a category, and then click a gallery swatch.

4. Click **OK** to apply the effect or fill to the object.

Editing the fill path

When you select a fillable object, the **Fill Tool** becomes available (otherwise it's greyed out). When you select the Fill Tool, if the object uses a **gradient fill**, you'll see the **fill path** displayed as a line, with nodes marking where the spectrum between each key colour begins and ends. Adjusting the node positions determines the actual spread of colours between nodes. You can also edit a gradient fill by adding, deleting, or changing key colours.

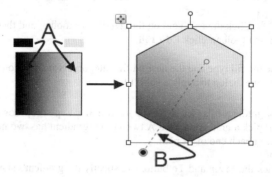

Linear Fill based on key colours   *Filled object showing fill path (B)*

(A)

To adjust the gradient fill path on a selected object:

1. Display the Swatches tab and ensure either ▬ Fill or ▬ Line is selected (for an object's fill or outline, respectively).

2. Click the ◈ **Fill Tool** on the **Attributes** toolbar. The fill path appears on the object's fill or outline.

3. Use the **Fill Tool** to drag the start and end path nodes, or click on the object for a new start node and drag out a new fill path. The gradient starts where you place the start node, and ends where you place the end node.

Each gradient fill type has a characteristic path. For example, Linear fills have single-line paths, while Radial fills have a two-line path so you can adjust the fill's extent in two directions away from the centre. If the object uses a **bitmap fill**, you'll see the fill path displayed as two lines joined at a centre point. Nodes mark the fill's centre and edges.

Working with transparency

Transparency effects are great for highlights, shading and shadows, and simulating "rendered" realism. They can make the critical difference between flat-looking publications and publications with depth and snap. PagePlus fully supports variable transparency and lets you apply solid, gradient, or bitmap transparency to an object's fill or outline easily.

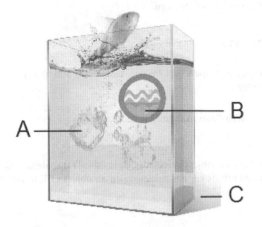

(A) bitmap transparency, (B) solid transparency, (C) gradient transparency

Transparencies work rather like fills that use "disappearing ink" instead of colour. The more transparency in a particular spot, the more "disappearing" takes place there, and the more the object(s) underneath show through. Just as a gradient fill can vary from light to dark, a transparency can vary from more to less, i.e. from clear to opaque, as in the illustration:

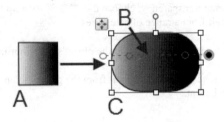

A - Linear Transparency, B - Path, C - Effect on Object

Transparency types available in the Transparency tab are as follows:

- **Solid** transparency distributes the transparency uniformly.

- **Gradient** transparencies include linear, elliptical, and conical effects, ranging from clear to opaque.

- **Bitmap** transparencies include categorized texture maps based on the Swatches tab's selection of bitmaps.

Applying transparency

You can apply transparency to shapes, text frames, table cells, and to any artistic, frame, and table text.

To apply transparency with Transparency tab:

1. With your object selected, display the Transparency tab and ensure either **Fill** or **Line** is selected (for an object's fill or outline, respectively).

2. For solid transparency, select the **Solid** button and pick a thumbnail from the solid transparency gallery. The lighter thumbnails represent more transparency (expressed as percentage).
   - or -

   For gradient transparency, choose the **Gradient** button and pick your thumbnail.
   - or -

   For bitmap transparency, choose the **Bitmap** button and pick a thumbnail from a range of categories.

3. The transparency is applied to the object's fill or outline.

Alternatively, drag the desired thumbnail from the gallery to an object, and release the mouse button.

To apply gradient transparency with the Transparency Tool:

1. Select the object and set the Transparency tab's Fill/Line swatch as before.

2. Click the Transparency Tool on the **Attributes** toolbar.

3. Drag your cursor across the object and release the mouse button. The object takes a simple Linear transparency, grading from 100% opacity to 0% opacity (fully transparent).

Editing transparency

Once you've applied a gradient transparency, you can adjust or replace its **path** on the object, and the **level** of transparency along the path. You can even create more complex transparency effects by adding extra nodes to the path by clicking and assigning different levels to each node.

To adjust the transparency path:

• Use the Transparency Tool to drag individual nodes, or click on the object for a new start node and drag out a new transparency path. The effect starts where you place the start node, and ends where you place the end node. For bitmap transparencies, the path determines the centre and two edges of the effect.

Editing a **gradient transparency** path is similar to editing a comparable fill path. Adding a level of transparency means varying the transparency gradient by introducing a new **node** and assigning it a particular value. For transparencies with multiple nodes, each node has its own value, comparable to a key colour in a gradient fill. Note that you cannot alter the values in a bitmap transparency.

To edit a gradient transparency directly:

1. Select the object and set the Transparency tab's **Fill/Line** swatch as before.

2. Click the ♀ **Transparency Tool** on the **Attributes** toolbar. The object's transparency path appears on the fill or line, with start and end nodes.

3. To **add** a transparency node, drag from any **solid transparency** sample in the Transparency tab to the point on the path where you want to add the node.

    The higher the percentage value assigned to a transparency node, the more transparent the effect at that point. Note: The hue of the colour doesn't matter, only its percentage value—so it's much easier just to choose from the set of gallery thumbnails.

4. To **change** the transparency value of any existing node, including the start and end nodes, select the node and click on a new thumbnail in the Transparency tab's Solid transparency gallery (you can also drag your chosen thumbnail onto the selected node).

5. To **move** a node you've added, simply drag it to a new position along the transparency path.

6. To **delete** a node you've added, select it and press **Delete**.

Setting the default transparency

The **default transparency** means the transparency that will be applied to the next new object you create. Local defaults only affect objects in the current project. For information on setting defaults in PagePlus, see Updating and saving defaults on p. 106.

10 Using PDF Forms

Getting started with PDF forms

PagePlus lets you use electronic-based PDF forms to collect inputted data from readers of your publication in an efficient and modern manner. In much the same way as traditional paper forms are used to collect information (remember your last Tax Return!), PDF forms offer the same form completion concepts, but increase the interaction between publisher and audience by using an electronic medium.

Some common form types include Application forms, Contact Information forms, Request forms, Feedback forms, and Guest books.

One thing in common with all PDF forms is that they have to be published as PDF to operate. A PagePlus .ppp file with form functionality must be converted to PDF with **Publish as PDF** (**Standard** toolbar).

Form Structure

The building blocks of a form comprise a mixture of text, graphics and **Form fields**. Form fields collect recipient data and can be added, moved and modified in a similar way to more familiar objects in PagePlus such as graphics and table elements. A field can be a Text field, Radio Button, Combo box, List box, Check box or a simple button.

From the form recipient's perspective, information is typed into text boxes or selected from check boxes, radio buttons, or drop-down boxes. The information entered can be numeric, textual, or a mixture of both. It is possible to arrange and lock form fields, plus control the order in which form fields can be navigated (see Designing your PDF forms in PagePlus Help).

Each field has its own set of **Form Field Properties** relating to its appearance, its value(s), validation, calculations, and the action expected of the field.

In PagePlus, the form should be integrated into your Page design as you develop your publication. The form's functionality only then becomes active when a PDF of the form is generated. When a form recipient enters data into form fields the data can be collected as described below.

JavaScript is used to allow interactivity in your PDF forms. It drives formatting, validation, calculations, and actions—all key functions in PDF form development.

How is data collected?

Several methods exist for collecting data from forms once they have been completed.

(1) By Hardcopy **Print.**

(2) You can **Save Data to e-mail** (alternatively you can save data within the form).

(3) You can **Submit Data to Web** (a CGI application; by submission to a web-enabled server/database).

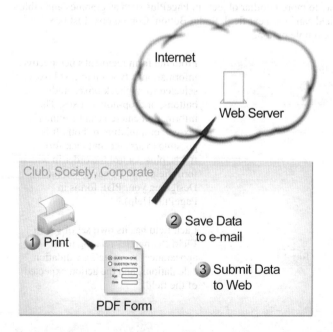

Creating PDF forms

Adding form fields

A series of form fields can be added to the page, depending on the type of form you want to create. Typically a mix of form fields will make up your finished form design.

Fields are created from the Form toolbar or via **Insert>Form Field**. You assign an internal unique name to each field and then set a variety of properties. Each form field has its own set of Form Field Properties which can be modified to suit your form implementation.

> The Form toolbar is turned off by default. Display it by going to **View>Toolbars>Form**.

> Form field names can contain "+", "-", "_", but no special characters.

Icon	Form Field Name	When to use?
	Button*	Use when specifying an action that can be triggered by a button click.
	Submit button*	Use when sending the form recipient's completed form data to Serif Web Resources or to your own Web server. A Form Submit Wizard is activated to enable quick and easy button setup.
	Reset button*	Use when you want to add a button to clear all form fields of data (often complements the above Submit button).
	Print button*	Use when you want to add a print button to your form.

* This button shares a drop down menu with other buttons marked with an asterisk. The button type previously chosen will always be displayed on the Form toolbar.

✓	Check Box	Ideal when you want to multiply select a series of options displayed side by side. A good alternative to a Combo Box or List box if space allows.
Ⅰ	Text Field	Use for adding text, numbers or a mixture of both.
▾	Combo Box	For selection from a scrollable list of items in a drop-down list where only one item can be selected. The box also allows data entry to be input into this box type. Smaller than a List Box.
1 2	List Box	For selection from a scrollable list of items; supports multiple selection and advanced actions on selection of menu items.
◉	Radio Button	Good for selection of a single mutually exclusive item from a grouped subset of choices.
✎	Signature	Used for the digital signing of secure documents. See PagePlus Help.
🔊	Sound Clip	Use to insert a PDF sound clip (.wav, .wave, .aif, .aiff, .aifc, .mp3).
🎬	Movie Clip	Use to insert a PDF movie clip (.avi, .flv, mpg, .mpeg, .mpe, .mpv, .mp4, .mpe4, .mov, .qt .swf).
▣	Form Field Properties	Use to view and edit the properties of the form fields.
1 2	Tab Order	Use to check or change the tab order of the fields.

To add a form field:

1. Select one of the form field buttons on the **Form** toolbar.

2. Move your ✛▦ cursor to the location at which you want to place your form field and click once.

3. Right-click on the form field and choose **Form Field Properties** from the drop-down list.

4. In the **General** tab, overwrite the current **Name** with a unique internal name. You can also choose several other optional settings (see PagePlus Help for more information).

5. Go to the **Options** tab. Depending on the field type, use this to enter list items, change the style, change the caption name and set defaults and other options.

6. (Optional) Go to the **Actions** tab and click the **Add** button.

7. (Optional) In the resulting Action dialog, select an Event that will be used to trigger the action.

8. (Optional) Choose an **Action** from the drop-down list.

9. (Optional) Change the properties displayed under the selected action. The options shown change depending on the action selected.

Form field properties

Form field properties control how the form field will operate when the form recipient enters their input. A series of tabs are arranged so that some tabs, e.g. **General, Appearance, Options,** or **Actions,** are common to all the form fields but others, such as **Format, Validate,** and **Calculate** are only displayed for text fields and combo boxes.

To access Form Field Properties:

1. To view the properties, do one of the following:

   - Right-click on a selected form field and choose **Form Field Properties...**.

   - Double-click the form field.

   - Select the form field, and click the ▣ button from the **Form** toolbar.

2. Click on one of several tabs for editing: General, Appearance, Options, Actions, Format, Validate, or Calculate.

3. Click the **OK** or **Cancel** button to exit the dialog.

Publishing your PDF Form

- Click ⬛ **Publish as PDF** on the **Standard** toolbar.

See Publishing PDF files on p. 261 for more information.

> If you Publish as PDF using PDF/X-1 or PDF/X-1a compatibility, any PDF form fields present will be converted to graphics and will not be available. Choose an Acrobat option instead.

Collecting data from forms

Via hardcopy printout

This is a simple fill-in and print to hardcopy solution. This is great if your form recipients are located together, perhaps in the same office.

> If using Adobe® Reader®, any completed form data will be lost when you close your completed PDF form. Exceptions exist when using Standard or Professional software.

Within the PDF file

Alternatively, it is possible to store form data within the PDF Form itself by using the **Save** or **Save As...** command. One condition of this is that the form recipient must be using Adobe® Acrobat® Professional (6.0 or later).

Using email

If you can save data within the PDF form then it's clear that you can email the completed form to the form originator. With the completed form still open, use **File>E-mail** to send the email to the intended recipient.

Via the web

Your PDF Form can be configured to be web ready by passing completed form data to a CGI application on a web server. This would typically be a server-sided web page designed to process the data and pass it to either a text file, database or other storage location. As an example, new subscriber details collected via a PDF Form can be sent automatically to a previously configured "subscribers" database.

All web-ready forms have one thing in common—they must be submitted to allow data to be collected. Typically, you may have come across this on web sites when you enter details into a form then submit the data by pressing a Submit button. The same applies for PDF forms—a **Submit** button can be configured in order to submit the form data to the web server. You can either create the button unaided or use the **Form Submit Wizard**. Either way, the use of the submit process is the major difference between web-ready and other less dynamic forms.

The web process, as mentioned, requires a web server to operate. Not everyone will have access to or even want to operate their own web server so, as an alternative to this, you can use **Serif Web Resources**. This is a free web to email gateway service which will collect your valued form data at Serif and send it to your email address—the service does require that you firstly have a Customer login (for security reasons), which will allow you to create, edit and delete Form IDs via a web page accessible from the Wizard. The Form ID, a unique alphanumeric code, is required for the service to operate and is generated automatically when you enter your destination email address in the above web page.

> No personal data will be stored on Serif web servers. All form data is redirected in real time.

Submitting Form Data

The submission of form data sounds like a very complicated operation but by using the **Form Submit Wizard**, the process is relatively straightforward. The Wizard not only creates a Submit button for your form, but configures the underlying submit process and the format in which your form data is to be stored in.

The submit process is made either to Serif Web Resources or to your own web server address (e.g., http://testserver.global.com/forms/collect.asp).

Form data can be stored in HTML, FDF, XFDF, and PDF data formats. See PagePlus Help for more details.

To run the Form Submit Wizard:

1. Select the 👆 **Submit Button** from the Button flyout menu on the **Form** toolbar.

2. In the first step, start the wizard by clicking the **Next>** button.

3. Choose either Serif Web Resources or your own server as the destination of your form recipient's data. The former is appropriate if you don't have access to your own web server. Depending on your choice, you can:

   1. **For Serif Web Resources**, click **Next>**.

   2. Click the **Get a Form ID** button to display Serif's customer login web page. This page is where you log onto your customer account to enter firstly your email address to send form data to, and secondly to generate a unique Form ID for use in the secure email communication.

   3. At the web page, if you already have a customer login you can enter your email address and password. If you are a new customer, you must register before continuing.

   4. Once logged in, select the **add new form** link to enter the email address that you want your form data to be sent to. You can also add a form description to help manage form IDs.

   5. Click the **Add Form** button. This generates an entry in the displayed list from which an alphanumeric Form ID code can be copied.

   6. Paste the Form ID directly from the web page into the input field in your Wizard dialog.

   7. Click the **Next>** button.

8. Select a Data format from the drop-down list that you would like to store and transport your form data. Select one of: HTML, FDF, or XFDF.

- or -

1. **For your own web server,** click **Next>**.

2. Add your Web Server address to the displayed field, click **Next>**. NOTE: this should not be a file directory but a valid website on the Intranet/Internet.

3. Choose a data format for exporting the form data. Select one of: HTML, FDF, PDF or XFDF. NOTE: You must ensure that your server is able to process the above data formats.

4. Finish the Wizard process by clicking the **Finish** button.

5. Move your cursor to the location for your button and click once.

11 Publishing and Sharing

Interactive Print/PDF Preview

The **Print/PDF Preview** mode changes the screen view to display your page layout without frames, guides, rulers, and other screen items. Supporting toolbars allow for a comprehensive and interactive preview of your publication pages before printing or publishing as PDF.

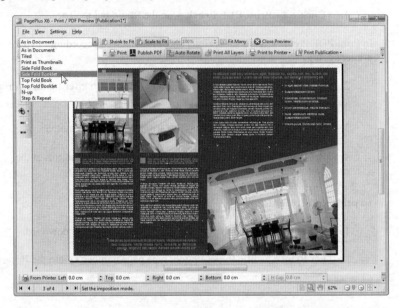

The Preview is interactive—its main feature is to provide dynamic **print-time imposition**. Put simply, this allows you to create folded books, booklets, and more, **at the printing/publication stage** from unfolded basic publication setups. Other interactive features are also available while in Preview mode.

- Select installed printers, and choose which pages to print and how they print (to printer, file or separation).

- Add and adjust printer margins.

- Switch on/off page marks when generating professional output.

- Control which database records print when using mail and photo merge via a Mail and Photo Merge toolbar.

Don't forget to make the most of the Preview's powerful **viewing controls** hosted on the View toolbar. Use zoom controls, Pan/Zoom tools, and multi-page views for detailed preview work.

To preview the page:

1. Click 🔳 **Print/PDF Preview** on the **Standard** toolbar.

In Print/PDF Preview, your first printer sheet is displayed according to your printer's setup.

2. (Optional) Choose an installed printer from the **Printer** toolbar's drop-down list.

3. (Optional) Adjust printer margins from the **Margins** toolbar.

4. Review your publication using the page navigation controls at the bottom of your workspace.

To print via Printer toolbar:

1. Choose which page to print via the **Print Range** drop-down list.

   For **Print Specific Pages** option, type page number(s) into the **Range** box.

2. Select 🖨 **Print**.

The standard **Print** dialog is then displayed, where settings are carried over from Preview mode (see Printing basics on p. 258).

To publish as PDF via Printer toolbar:

• Select 🅰 **Publish PDF**.

The standard **Publish PDF** dialog is then displayed (see Publishing PDF files on p. 261).

To cancel Preview mode:

- Select 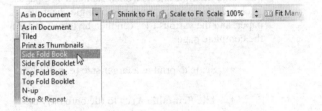 **Close Preview** from the top of your workspace.

Document imposition in Preview mode

During preview, you can enable imposition of your document, choosing a mode suited to your intended final publication (book, booklet, etc.). Each mode displays different toolbar options on the context-sensitive **Imposition** toolbar. Document imposition is not limited to desktop printing—it can also be used when creating a press-ready PDF for professional printing.

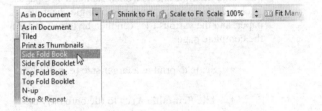

To choose an imposition mode:

- From the **Imposition** toolbar, select an option from the **Imposition Mode** drop-down list.

As in Document	Select to print/publish pages as they appear in your document, i.e. one page per sheet. Scaling options include:
	• **Shrink to fit** to reduce the page to the printer sheet size.
	• **Scale to fit** to adjust artwork automatically to fit neatly on the printed/published page, taking printer margins into account.
	• **Scale** to specify a custom scaling. The default is 100% or normal. Specify a larger or smaller value to print/publish at a larger or smaller size, respectively.

	• If you haven't set up the publication as a Small Publication, but still want to include multiple pages per sheet, try using **Fit Many**. Note: this option ignores printer margins and doesn't change the imposition (orientation) of output pages. For printing, ensure your page layout borders don't extend beyond the printable region.
Tiled	Even if the publication isn't set up as a **poster** or **banner**, you can use tiling and scaling settings to print onto multiple sheets from a standard size page. Each section or tile is printed on a single sheet of paper, and the various tiles can then be joined to form the complete page. • **Scale** to print at a larger size (e.g. 300%). • **Tile Printable Area** to tile onto only the printable area of the sheet. • **Tile Overlap** to simplify arrangement of the tiles and to allow for printer margins.
Print as Thumbnails	Select to add multiple pages at a reduced size on each sheet, taking printer margins into account. • Set the number of thumbnails per sheet in the **Per Sheet** box. PagePlus will print/publish each page of the publication at a reduced size, with the specified number of small pages or "thumbnails" neatly positioned on each sheet.
Side Fold Book	Select to paginate as a side fold book, optionally using scaling options described above.
Side Fold Booklet	Select to paginate as a side fold booklet, optionally using scaling options described above.

Top Fold Book	Select to paginate as a top fold book, optionally using scaling options described above.
Top Fold Booklet	Select to paginate as a top fold booklet, optionally using scaling options described above.
N-up/N-up Repeat	Select to paginate with multiple pages per sheet, with each page repeating a configurable number of times. • **Across** sets the number of copies across the page. • **Down** sets the number of copies down the page. • **Repeat** selects the number of times to repeat each page. • **Skip** lets you omit a certain number of regions on the first sheet of paper. Skipping regions is useful when printing and, for example, you've already peeled off several labels from a label sheet, and don't want to print on the peeled-off sections. • **Fill Last Page** will populate the last page with your repeating region rather than just printing/publishing an almost blank page.
Step & Repeat	Select to paginate with multiple pages per sheet, with each sheet containing copies of the same page only. • **Across** sets the number of copies across the page. • **Down** sets the number of copies down the page.

Printing books and booklets

To produce double-sided sheets, click 🖨 **Print** and use the Print dialog's Double-sided Printing or Manual Duplex options (under More Options). Ensure your printer is setup for double-sided printing or run sheets through twice, printing first the front and then the back of the sheet (reverse top and bottom between runs). The sheets can then be collated and bound at their centre to produce a booklet, with all the pages in the correct sequence.

Printing basics

Printing your publication to a desktop printer is one of the more likely operations you'll be performing in PagePlus. The easy-to-use Print dialog presents the most commonly used options to you, with a navigable "live" Preview window to check your print output.

The dialog also supports additional printing options via the **More Options** button including **Double-sided Printing**, **Mail Merge**, **Rasterize**, and many other useful printing options. One particular option, called **Layout**, allows for print-time imposition of your publication—simply create a booklet or other folded publication at the print stage.

For a detailed description of each option, see PagePlus Help.

Here we'll cover what you need to know for basic desktop printer output. If you're working with a service bureau or professional printer and need to provide PDF output, see Publishing PDF files (p. 261) and Generating professional output (see PagePlus Help).

To set up your printer or begin printing:

1. (Optional) To print selected text or objects, make your selection on the page.

2. Click ⬛ **Print** on the **Standard** toolbar. The Print dialog appears.

3. Select a currently installed printer from the **Printer** drop-down list. If necessary, click the **Properties** button to set up the printer for the correct page size, etc.

4. Select a printer profile from the **Profile** drop-down list. You can just use **Current Settings** or choose a previously saved custom profile (.ppr) based on a combination of dialog settings; **Browse...** lets you navigate to any .ppr file on your computer. To save current settings, click the **Save As...** button, and provide a unique profile name. The profile is added to the drop-down list.

> ✦ If you modify any profile settings, an asterisk appears next to the profile name.

5. Select the number of copies to print, and optionally instruct the printer to **Collate** them.

6. Select the print **Range** to be printed, e.g. the Entire Publication, Current Page, Current Selection (if selected text or objects in step 1), or range of pages. For specific pages or a range of pages, enter "1,3,5" or "2-5", or enter any combination of the two.

   Whichever option you've chosen, the **Include** drop-down list lets you export all sheets in the range, or just odd or even sheets, with the option of printing in **Reverse** order.

7. Set a percentage **Scale** which will enlarge or shrink your print output (both page and contents). A 100% scale factor creates a full size print output. Alternatively, from the adjacent drop-down list, choose **Shrink to Fit** to reduce your publication's page size to the printer sheet size or **Scale to Fit** to enlarge or reduce the publication page size as required.

8. Keep **Auto Rotate** checked if you want your publication page to automatically rotate your printer's currently set sheet orientation. When you access the Print dialog, if page and sheet sizes do not match, you'll be prompted to adjust your printer sheet orientation automatically (or you can just ignore auto-rotation).

9. Select an option from the **Work around printer problems** drop-down list. **Best Quality** is selected by default, but occasionally problems arise with some printer drivers when bitmaps in a publication use transparency. If you are getting poor results, you can select the **Send As Bitmap** option to output whole pages as bitmaps. While slower, this approach virtually guarantees successful printing.

10. Click **Print**.

More print options

Additional print options are available from the Print dialog if you're planning to use imposition at print time (see p. 253), use specific PagePlus features which use printing (e.g., Mail Merge), print double-sided, or generate professional output.

Publishing PDF files

PagePlus can output your drawings to PDF (Portable Document Format), a cross-platform WYSIWYG file format developed by Adobe, intended to handle documents in a device- and platform-independent manner.

PDF documents are ideal for both **web-ready** distribution and **professional** printing.

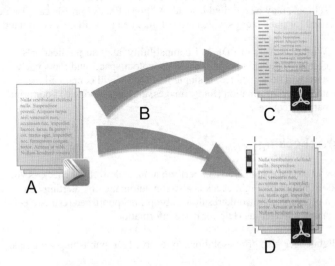

(A) PagePlus Publication, (B) Preflight and Publish, (C) web-ready PDF, (D) Press-ready PDF (professional).

In PagePlus, ready-to-go PDF profiles are available for both uses, making PDF setup less complicated.

- **Web-ready**. If you require web-ready PDFs you're likely to need PDF documents which are optimized for screen use, i.e. with hyperlinks, downsampled images, document security, but without pre-press page marks, bleed, etc. Downsampling images leads to smaller documents for quicker loading.

  Profiles such as "Web - Compact" and "Web - Normal" are provided for web-ready use (downsampling images to 96 and 150dpi, respectively), and are ideal for hosting PDFs on websites or other electronic distribution (email).

- **Professional.** PDF documents are suited to professional printing, i.e. when you deliver a high quality reproduction of your drawing to a print partner (normally external to your company). You'll typically require page marks, bleed, ≥300dpi images, and PDF/X-1a compatibility (for CMYK output).

  To make things simple, the professional print profile called "PDF X-1a" is provided in PagePlus (using PDF X-1a compatibility), but you should check with your print partner if PDF/X-1, and any other settings, may be required instead. A "Press Ready" profile can also be used for publications which are not intended to be PDF/X compliant.

  With PDF/X-1a or PDF/X-1 compatibility, all your publication's colours will be output in the CMYK colour space, and fonts you've used will be embedded. A single PDF/X file will contain all the necessary information (fonts, images, graphics, and text) your print partner requires.

Preflight checking

To assist you as you design, you can perform a manual preflight check as you go. On publishing, a preflight check is also run automatically, alerting you to any design problems that would result in sub-optimal published results. See Preflight check in PagePlus Help for more information.

The preflight check also offers solutions to resolve PDF publishing warnings.

Publishing a PDF

To publish as a PDF file:

1. Prepare the publication following standard print publishing guidelines, and taking the distribution method into account.

2. (Optional) Insert text hyperlinks and TOC hyperlinks as needed.

3. (Optional) Once the publication is final, prepare a bookmark list (see Creating a PDF bookmark list on p. 263).
   Note: Bookmarks appear as a separate list in a special pane when the PDF file is viewed. They can link to a specific page or to an **anchor** (for example, a piece of text or a graphic object) in your publication.

4.   Click 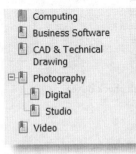 **Publish as PDF** on the **Standard** toolbar.

5.   From the dialog, check your export settings. For a detailed explanation of each export setting see PagePlus Help.

6.   Click **OK** to proceed to export.

If you checked **Preview PDF file** (General tab), the resulting PDF file appears in the default PDF reader installed on your system.

Creating a PDF bookmark list

Bookmarks are optional links that appear in a separate pane of the Adobe Reader when a PDF file is displayed.

Typically, a bookmark links to a specific location such as a section heading in the publication, but it can also link to a whole page or specifically to an anchor attached to an object. You can insert bookmarks by hand, or PagePlus can apply **automatic generation** to produce a nested bookmark list up to six levels deep, derived from named styles in your publication.

You'll be able to view all your bookmarks at a glance, organize them into a hierarchy of entries and subentries, and create, modify or delete existing bookmarks as needed.

To use styles to automatically generate bookmarks:

1. Select **PDF Bookmarks...** from the **Insert** menu.

2. In the dialog, click **Automatic...**. You'll see a list of all the style names available to PagePlus. Check boxes to include text of a given style as a heading at a particular level (1 through 6). For example, for Heading 1, Heading 2, and Heading 3 at three hierarchical levels:

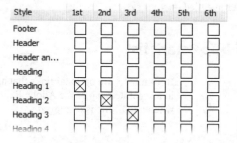

To remove all bookmarks in the list, clear all check boxes.

3. Click **OK** to generate bookmarks.

The mechanics of **creating a PDF bookmark list by hand** are simple. For example, bookmarking a specific location (for example, a piece of text or a graphic object) entails placing an **anchor** at that location; the anchor serves as the target for the bookmark link.

To insert bookmarks by hand:

1. Select **PDF Bookmarks...** from the **Insert** menu.

2. In the bookmark tree, display the entry below which you want to create the new bookmark. (Check **Create as sub-entry** if you want the new bookmark nested as a "child" of the selected entry.)

3. Click the **Create...** button.

4. In the Create Bookmark dialog, type the text for your bookmark in the **Bookmark Title** field. This text will be displayed in Adobe Reader as the bookmark name.

5. Click to select the bookmark destination type, then enter the
    destination.

- To bookmark a specific page in the publication, set **Destination
  Type** to be **Page**, then select the target page's **Page Number**.

- To bookmark to a specific location, set **Destination Type** to be
  Anchor, then select the target anchor's **Anchor Name**.

6. Click **OK** to confirm your choices.

> You'll need to have created an anchor in advance to allow it to be
> bookmarked. You can create PDF bookmarks automatically when
> creating anchors. (See Adding anchors to objects on p. 97.)

To delete bookmarks:

1. Select **PDF Bookmarks...** from the **Insert** menu.

2. In the bookmark tree, select an entry for deletion, then click the
    Remove button. You'll be asked if you want to remove unused
    anchors.

> A bookmark, if using an anchor, can also be deleted when the anchor is
> deleted (via **Insert>Anchor...**).

Unlike hyperlinks, bookmarks also work as actual links within PagePlus
publications. You can use the bookmark list as a jumping-off point to any
bookmarked entry.

Publishing as eBooks

The emergence of eBooks in recent years offers not just the traditional book publishers an opportunity to explore new electronic book markets, but also provides the writer with the ability to publish their own eBooks.

In PagePlus, you can be your own publisher and create eBooks in both ePub and mobi formats. Like publishing to PDF and HTML, the process of eBook publishing is straightforward, with the added benefit of manual and automatic preflight checking to ensure your file conforms to eBook standards.

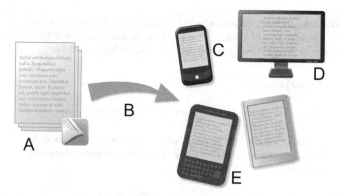

(A) PagePlus Publication, (B) Preflight and Publish, (C) Android phone, (D) Computer, (E) Kindle/ePub readers.

PagePlus and eBook publishing

EBooks by their nature, are intended to display stories that reflow text content throughout your book. As a result, the PagePlus user should bear in mind what they can reasonably expect to output as an eBook. Complex page layouts are not suited to eBook publishing, while simple layouts focused on a single flowing text frame are perfect (remember that you can flow text across multiple pages using the same text frame in PagePlus!). For example, a publication based on a design template (with freely placed pictures and artistic text) would not be a good candidate for eBook publishing. Instead, if you start a publication from scratch, you'll be in a better position to conform to eBook standards.

One other key factor in successful eBook publishing is the use of regimented heading text styles, typically Heading, Heading 1, and Heading 2, assigned to your headings. Some complex page layouts dispense with these hierarchical heading styles, but in eBook publishing these headings are important to identify your eBook chapters.

To help you prepare for eBook publishing, the following design tips and tricks should assist you in getting started.

Design tips and tricks

If you plan to create eBooks effortlessly there are several useful do's and don'ts that you should bear in mind during eBook design.

When designing eBooks, do:

- Pre-plan your eBook's design in advance of publishing.

- Keep your story contained within text frames. Optionally edit your frame's story text in WritePlus, allowing you to paste content, import text and develop the story in isolation.

- Use pre-supplied heading text styles in your story.

- Create a cover for your eBook as a picture.

- Create a single TOC.

Conversely, don't:

- Place any object (picture, artistic, header/footer text, etc.) outside the main text frame.

- Anchor floating objects to your text frame. Anchored inline objects are acceptable.

- Create excessively long chapters (<300k is recommended).

For more help about optimizing Amazon Kindle publishing, see the **Amazon Kindle Publishing Guidelines** at http://www.amazon.com/kindlepublishing/

Preflight checking

To assist you as you design, you can perform a manual preflight check as you go. On publishing, a preflight check is also run automatically, alerting you to any design problems that would result in sub-optimal published results. See Preflight check in PagePlus Help for more information.

The preflight check also offers solutions to resolve eBook publishing warnings.

Publishing

Two approaches can be taken depending on which devices you intend to publish for, i.e. to ePub or Kindle. Both publishing processes are similar, except that they create different file formats (i.e., *.epub and *.mobi, respectively). Kindle publishing additionally requires the KindleGen program to be installed on your computer.

To publish an eBook for ePub devices:

1. Choose **Publish As>** from the **File** menu and select **eBook...** from the submenu.

2. From the dialog's Document Info menu, add metadata, an ID, and a pre-designed eBook cover (if needed).

3. With the Output menu item selected, control how tables, lists, and pictures are to be exported.

4. With the Styles menu item selected, you can control how your publication's currently used text styles affect your eBook after publishing. Select a text style from the list, then select an **Action for this style**.

5. Click **OK**.

6. In the **Publish eBook** dialog, navigate to the location where you wish to publish your eBook, then enter a file name in the **File name** box. Keep the **Save as type** drop-down list set to "ePub files (*.epub)".

7. Click **Save**.

To publish an eBook for Kindle:

1. Install the KindleGen program, downloadable from Amazon Kindle publishing.

2. Follow the procedure as for ePub devices above.

3. In the dialog's Output menu, under the Kindle section, click **Browse...** to navigate to (and select) the kindlegen.exe file from the installed folder above.

4. Click **OK**.

5. From the **Publish eBook** dialog, navigate to a folder, choose a filename, and change the **Save as type** drop-down list to "Kindle files (*.mobi)".

6. Click **Save**.

If you checked **Show document after publication**, the ePub book will launch in its associated reader.

> If you've not already downloaded KindleGen, click **Download KindleGen from Amazon....** This takes you directly to the Amazon Kindle publishing website.

Previewing Kindle

Any kindle book (*.mobi) you create can be previewed on your computer if either you don't possess a Kindle device (or it's unavailable) or you need to check it before transfer to your Kindle device (or upload to Amazon). To do so you need to install Kindle Previewer software available from Amazon Kindle publishing.

Displaying your eBook

Once you've published your eBook you'll want to make it available to a physical device as soon as possible. Typical ways that your eBook can be read, include:

- Via **computer**: Install Adobe Digital Editions software to view your ePub document. Similarly, Kindle Previewer software is the choice for Kindle files.

- Via **Kindle/Android phone**: Transfer your published *.mobi file by copying to your device via your USB port. Alternatively, you can send your file via email directly to your device.

- Via **ePub physical device/Android phone**: Like Kindle devices, you can transfer your *.epub file to your device via USB.

> Transfer of eBooks to physical devices is outside the scope of PagePlus Help. Consult your device's supporting documentation for details.

Like in HTML publishing, you can select an object and force it to be converted to a picture on publishing. You would do this to ensure conformance to ebook standards, perhaps after a failed preflight check.

Publishing as HTML

PagePlus allows you to publish any publication as separate HTML pages, ready for the web. One advantage PagePlus has over a dedicated web-page creation program is that you can take your newsletter layout, or a print ad with a wild mix of multi-colour graphics and fancy typography, and publish them ready for upload to the web.

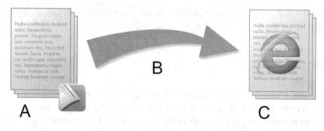

(A) PagePlus Publication, (B) Preflight and Publish, (C) HTML pages.

To publish to the **web**, you'll need a host for your website—that is, disk space on a server connected to the Internet—so that others can access your site. This usually means opening an account with an online service provider: either your Internet service provider (ISP) providing dedicated web space, or a specialized/independent web hosting provider. The big subscription networks typically allocate to each user a generous amount of server web space for your website. Once you've set up your account, all that's needed is to transfer your published HTML files to your online web space. Consult with your provider about the best way to transfer files to your web space.

To ensure your HTML pages appear in your website as intended, a preflight check is automatically carried out to identify (and often correct) text-specific problems, objects that will export as graphics, overlapping objects, non-WebSafe fonts, or other conditions that will result in file sizes that are larger than necessary.

Creating a web publication

To create a new web publication from scratch:

1. Launch PagePlus or choose **New>New from Startup Wizard** from the **File** menu.

2. In the Startup Wizard, select **Start New Publication**.

3. From the dialog, select **Custom Page Setup...**.

4. Enable **Regular/Booklet Publication**, and enter your web page dimensions in the **Width** and **Height** boxes. Remember to specify dimensions in pixels (e.g., as 600 pix).

5. Click **OK**.

Preflight checking

To assist you as you design, you can perform a manual preflight check as you go. On publishing, a preflight check is also run automatically, alerting you to any design problems that would result in sub-optimal published results. See Preflight check in PagePlus Help for more information.

The preflight check also offers solutions to resolve HTML publishing warnings.

Publishing

Publishing the site to a local disk folder lets you preview the pages in your own browser prior to uploading your pages to your online web space. You'll be able to keep your browser program open, and go back and forth between PagePlus and the browser each time your publish. This way you can make changes to a single page in PagePlus, publish just the one page, then switch to your browser and preview that page to make sure everything appears just as you want it.

To publish as HTML:

1. Choose **Publish As>** from the **File** menu and select **HTML...** from the submenu.

2. From the dialog, set general export options (including browser choice) and global hyperlink, on-page, and background colours. You can also control how graphics are exported.

3. In the **Publish to Disk Folder** dialog, either paste the location where you wish to store your output files in the **Output** box or click **Choose Folder...** to navigate to an existing folder.

4. Either keep the **Publish All Pages** option checked, or in the site structure tree, check which specific page(s) to publish. The latter will save a lot of time by skipping the export of pages you haven't changed.

5. Click **OK**.

After PagePlus has finished exporting the selected pages, you'll be asked if you want to launch your web browser to view your page. Click **Yes** if you wish to do this.

> Hyperlink colours are global, but you'll be able to override on-page and background colours for specific pages by right-clicking a page and selecting **Page Properties....**

Setting up your webspace

It's up to you to establish an account you can use to host your published HTML output. You'll need to transfer your HTML output to your web space once this is done.

Your ISP (Internet Service Provider) may offer web space for you to upload to, or you could use a separate web hosting provider independent of your ISP. Contact your ISP or web hosting provider for further information.

Adding page titles

To aid page identification, a web page **title** can be added to the page which will appear in the title bar of the visitor's web browser.

To enter a title for the current web page:

1. Right-click a page and select **Page Properties...**

2. In the **Title** box enter a page title, e.g, Welcome.

General options

Additional global options can be set, which affect all published pages equally. It's a good idea to check these as your ISP may require specific settings (e.g., html file names only).

Colour options

Hyperlink colours, on-page colour, background colour, and your background image can be set globally as you publish to HTML. This means all your created web pages will adopt these settings, although you have the option to override on-page and background settings per page. See Setting page properties in PagePlus Help.

By default, publications based on a template or those created from scratch use schemed colours for their hyperlink and on-page colours, but these will need to be set on HTML publishing. These colours belong to the publications's current colour scheme but you can swap to a different scheme or change the individual colours at any time. See Using colour schemes on p. 223.

To set hyperlink, on-page and background colours:

1. Choose **Publish As>** from the **File** menu and select **HTML...** from the submenu.

2. From the dialog's **Colours** menu option, click the down arrow for the hyperlink, on-page, or background colour you want to change.

3. Select a different colour from the flyout, which shows numbered scheme colours and other colours. Select **More Colour...** to optionally pick from a Colour Selector dialog.

4. Click **OK**.

To set a background image:

1. From the dialog's **Colours** menu option, click **Background Image....**

2. Check **Use Background Image**, then locate and select the image from the Import Picture dialog. Click **Open**. Use **Browse...** to swap your image at any time.

3. Click **OK**.

Graphic options

When you publish to HTML, PagePlus applies certain global settings to determine how each image—whether drawn, pasted in, or imported—ends up as a separate bitmap in your output folder.

The following conversion settings are used during publishing to HTML:

*   Any inserted GIF, JPEG, or PNG image is published in its original file format, but with an automatically generated file name, e.g. pp34534a1ca06.jpg.

*   Inserted metafiles and all other graphics are converted to PNG images, again generating new file names.

You can alter these settings, but before doing so you should review the "logic" PagePlus applies to publishing web graphics. Global publishing options and setting output formats are described in more detail in the PagePlus Help.

Sharing by email

PagePlus lets you share publications as native PagePlus publications (.ppp) or as HTML, as a file attachment or as HTML within the body of your email, respectively.

To share PagePlus publications:

1. With your publication open and in the currently active window, select **Send...** from the **File** menu.

   If you have multiple email programs and they are not loaded, a Choose Profile dialog lets you select your email program of choice, then a new email message is displayed with document attached. If already loaded, your email program automatically attaches your publication to a new email message.

2. Add the recipient's valid email address to the **To...** field (or equivalent).

3. Select the **Send** button (or equivalent) on your email program as for any other email message.

> An Internet connection is required for the emailing of publications.

Sharing PagePlus publications as HTML or images

Interested in sharing content with recipients who may not be using PagePlus? **Send page as HTML** lets you dispatch any page as HTML or as a bitmap. For HTML, all referenced images and hyperlinks are embedded locally with the message. For sharing as a bitmap, the message will be larger but will guarantee that the document will appear as intended (great for ensuring compatibility with older email clients).

Normally, an installed email client such as Outlook will be used by default. However, if you don't have an installed email program or have Office (but don't want to use it), you can use PagePlus to act as an email client instead. The only prerequisite is having an outgoing SMTP mail server to transfer the email to—you'll need to know the server address in advance.

To use PagePlus as an alternative email client:

- Select **Tools>Options...**, then select **HTML E-mail**.

- Enable **Send HTML E-mail using PagePlus**, and enter the mail server name (e.g., mail-srv or mail.company.com). The port number 25 is always used.

> Both HTML and image sharing methods share a single page only. To share a multi-page publication with recipients who don't use PagePlus, consider outputting your project as a PDF and then send the PDF as an attachment.

To share a document as an HTML page:

1. With your publication open, select the page you would like to send.

2. Select **Send Page as HTML...** from the **File** menu. The page is added to the body of a newly created HTML-based email message.

3. Add the recipient's valid email address to the **To...** field (or equivalent).

4. Select the **Send** button (or equivalent) on your email program.

> Use this option for Outlook Express, Outlook (pre-Outlook 2007), and Windows Mail.

To share a document as an image:

1. Check **Send entire HTML page as single image** in Tools>Options>User Interface>HTML E-mail (in PagePlus).

2. Carry out procedure as for sharing a document as HTML above.

> Use this option for Outlook Express, Outlook, and Windows Mail.

Notes

Notes

Notes

Notes